Zouch H Turton

To the Desert and back

or, Travels in Spain, the Barbary States, Italy, etc., in 1875-6

Zouch H Turton

To the Desert and back
or, Travels in Spain, the Barbary States, Italy, etc., in 1875-6

ISBN/EAN: 9783337038953

Printed in Europe, USA, Canada, Australia, Japan

Cover: Foto ©ninafisch / pixelio.de

More available books at **www.hansebooks.com**

TO THE DESERT AND BACK;

OR,

Travels in Spain, the Barbary States, Italy, etc.,

IN 1875—6.

BY

ZOUCH H. TURTON.

London:
SAMUEL TINSLEY,
10, SOUTHAMPTON STREET, STRAND.
1876.

[*All rights reserved.*]

CONTENTS.

CHAP.		PAGE
I.	LONDON TO THE SPANISH FRONTIER	1
II.	FROM BAYONNE TO VALLADOLID	15
III.	AVILA AND THE ESCORIAL	31
IV.	MADRID AND TOLEDO	43
V.	CORDOVA AND SEVILLE	60
VI.	CADIZ AND GIBRALTAR	75
VII.	TANGIER	86
VIII.	MALAGA	96
IX.	GRANADA	108
X.	VALENCIA AND BARCELONA	121
XI.	ORAN	133
XII.	A NIGHT WITH ARABS	142
XIII.	MOSTAGANEM TO ALGIERS	157
XIV.	ALGIERS	168
XV.	BOUGIE TO SETIF	176
XVI.	CONSTANTINE	185
XVII.	THE DESERT	193
XVIII.	BATNA TO TUNIS	211
XIX.	TUNIS	222
XX.	SICILY	233
XXI.	NAPLES	242
XXII.	ROME TO MENTONE	260
XXIII.	MENTONE TO LONDON	270
XXIV.	STATISTICS AND FINANCES	280

TO THE DESERT AND BACK.

CHAPTER I.

LONDON TO THE SPANISH FRONTIER.

Littlehampton—Crossing the Channel—French Towns—Our Engine—Tours and its Sights—Poitiers—Old Churches—Bordeaux—Arcachon and Biarritz—The Frontier—Carlists and Alphonsists—Return to Bayonne.

On a fine morning towards the end of July we—myself and brother—left Victoria station, for a tour in Spain. Our first detention was at Littlehampton—a fishy-looking town which we saw in about half-an-hour; and then boarded a small steamer lying in the river, advertised to start for Honfleur at 4 p.m.

When 4 p.m. came, there was a slight disagreement between ourselves and the tide—the latter getting the better of the argument; so we had to shelve in, and quietly put off our departure for an hour. At 5 p.m., we and the tide being then *en rapport*, anchor was weighed, and a start made. A heavy swell soon sent many of the passengers into a contemplative mood; which, in a good many instances, was followed by a state not quite so tranquil. Everyone knows the scenes that occur on board ship soon after a passenger vessel faces the waves; but let us not dwell on unpleasant reminiscences—unpleasant for those who suffer, as well as for those who, like myself, simply behold it in others.

About nine, most of us descended into a small cabin, which—on the steward's information—was made to contain twenty-one persons. Otherwise, we should have thought ten over-crowding; and had it concerned sheep, it would have called for the intervention of some Humane Society. The ladies' cabin was in the fore-part of the vessel; but being still more uninviting, they were allowed to share the one I have referred to, which was intended exclusively for male occupants. "Give an inch, take an ell:"— when I went down in the course of the evening, to get something out of my portmanteau, one of them actually had the face to ask me what right I had there! I meekly replied that I had only come to fetch my flask. She went upstairs to consult the steward: what he said, I fancy, did not please her; for she came back, looking daggers, and as sulky as a bear. This put me in mind of the man who said, "Sister, I am very hungry, and the loaf is very small; but you're welcome to half."

"What business have you to keep *any*?" she curtly replied. "Don't you know that I am a lady?"

An Egyptian Jew once showed me the morning prayers of his race; in them was a petition: "God preserve me from ever being a woman!" Amen! and so let us close the subject, and try to sleep; for the shades of night have long since drawn in.

Early the next morning, the French coast

was to be seen by those who were on deck, and wished to get a glimpse of La Belle France; but we preferred sleeping on, until we reached Honfleur, when there was a general turn out, all being glad enough, I have no doubt, to exchange the limited accommodations enjoyed on board, for the freedom of *terra firma*.

As there is nothing worth staying for in Honfleur, we left immediately for Lisieux, where we breakfasted, and then went in search of a money-changer; seeing, *en route*, two handsome churches, and smelling rather more than two perfectly distinct and equally obnoxious smells; returning to the railway station, in time to catch the Le Mans train, which starts at ten.

A very long tunnel was passed, and several hours spent in a carriage which might, without much exaggeration, be compared to a heated oven—so intense were the rays of the sun on that day.

No one who ever comes to Le Mans, should miss seeing the choir of its cathedral

—a masterpiece of Gothic art. It is difficult to say whether the richly-coloured interior, or the profusely pinnacled exterior, is the more beautiful.

After dinner we started for Tours, determined to get over this part of the journey with as little delay as possible. When we had taken our seats in the train, the engine whistled the hoarsest whistle I have ever heard. Poor thing! It seemed to be suffering from bronchitis; and we felt that it was quite a shame to work it, instead of sending it to the engine-house. My brother suggested, "Perhaps it was only shamming;" so with this consoling reflection, we dismissed the subject, and looked at the country, which became more verdant as we travelled south. About 10 p.m., our bronchial engine, having made a last feeble attempt at a whistle, drew us into the venerable city of Tours, where we passed the rest of the night in oblivion.

Shrine of S. Martin! I had pictured myself kneeling before all that is mortal of the once bishop and confessor—imagination had brought before me the ancient abbey with its vaulted roof, soft music floating through its aisles, and the fumes of incense wafted around. But alas for earthly hopes and expectations! The revolution has done its work; two towers alone tell where the abbey once stood, and Tours no longer boasts of her proudest relic—the bones of S. Martin are scattered to the winds.

Let us turn, *faute de mieux*, to the cathedral, and admire its noble *façade*, and the stained glass of its choir. Mass was being celebrated as we entered, and I could not help noticing the reverence alike of people and clergy—a marked contrast to what is usual in Spain and Italy.

The remaining sights of Tours, are the church of Notre Dame la Riche, containing some curious figures—the two towers of the abbey already alluded to, the distance between them giving some idea of its former size—the house in which Tristan l'Hermite, executioner to Louis XI., lived—a handsome bridge—and, some way out of the town, the ruins of the Abbey of Marmoutier; which, like the celebrated Chinese wall, are only to be seen if in the neighbourhood, and hardly repay a two miles walk along a dusty road.

Tours was one of the last towns which *M.M. les Prussiens* thought it their painful duty to occupy. During our stay it was blessed with a hot sun and a cold wind—an unpleasant combination which we did not altogether relish; so taking the train the second day after our arrival, and travelling for three hours through a prettily wooded and undulating country, we reached our next halt.

The external appearance of Poitiers pleased us much. It is situated on an eminence, and has many objects of interest both in the town and neighbourhood. The church of S. Hilaire, which has recently been very much enlarged, and was scarcely finished at the time of our visit, is of ancient foundation, and contains a curious sarcophagus of the 8th century, lying immediately under the high altar, in a sort of *confessio;* also a *bénitier* of somewhat older date—probably one of the first introduced.

The Temple de S. Jean—a structure whose completion could not have been later, according to most authorities, than the 7th century, when erected for a baptistery—has nothing to recommend it externally; and buildings of later date have so surpassed it, both in size and elegance, that antiquity is its only merit.

We next visited the Abbey of S. Radegonde. The excited state of those within and without, led us to infer that a procession was just about to start on its rounds. Several old women were very anxious that we should buy tapers; but not feeling disposed to promenade about the streets with a lighted candle, we declined.

The cathedral, which has a fine *façade*, is of the 12th century. After hearing mass, we went in search of the demi-dolman, about a mile and a half distant. It is a very good specimen of its kind; and, from the size of the stones, affords a striking proof of the motive powers which must have been known to the ancients. These monuments, attributed to the Druids, have been long thought pre-historic; but are believed on more recent investigation to have been erected not earlier than the Christian era —probably to commemorate some victory.

The country between Poitiers and Bordeaux is well wooded, and presents an appearance which is best described as "smiling." Here every field is a park; every waste patch of ground a garden. The episcopal city of Angoulême lies midway. Then vineyards herald the approach of Bordeaux.

As the temperature had been about 80° the last few days,—with but a very slight abatement in our favour during the night— we were rather gratified to find that we had to see Bordeaux on a cloudy day. Bending our steps across the celebrated bridge which here spans the Garonne, to its left bank, we came upon the beautiful church of S. Michel, which, together with that of S. Croix and the cathedral, is amongst the finest in the town. The stained glass in all is one of their most effective features. The former cathedral of S. Severin was, this morning, strewn with leaves, and filled with people; many of whom were using their chairs to stand upon, in order to get a better view of what was going forward. A large band, composed of wind and stringed instruments, was performing in such a way as to lead one to suppose that noise was the only object desired. Mass was being celebrated at the time; but the band seemed to have no connection with the service, playing on uninterruptedly, much in the style of Oriental musicians.

Bordeaux has some fine arches, and a public garden. Passing the quay, we saw a number of men of a half Portugese, half Brazilian cut; and in several of the shops, notices to the effect that Spanish was there spoken. We felt ourselves, at last, on the confines of Spain; and rejoicing in this reflection, returned home.

Between this and Bayonne, hardly any trees are to be seen, except the pine, which flourishes in every direction. Arcachon, which is not on the open sea, but on a small inlet, is a pretty place—as indeed any place would be when there is a combination of wood and water, affording shady walks and fine sea-bathing. It is principally frequented by the rich of Bordeaux, strangers being less common than in Biarritz. Here we noticed the curious custom of the sexes bathing together, each habited in a becoming costume. A great deal has been said about the Egyptian look of Arcachon; but I failed to observe it. Possibly it is only to be noticed by those who have not been in Egypt.

Bayonne, the next place of importance on the route, contains the usual complement to be found in a French town; the military element predominating. The streets are narrow; oxen are used equally with horses for drawing burdens, and two or three mongrel curs turn up at every corner.

Five miles south of this, is the fashionable watering-place of Biarritz—a truly delightful spot; presenting a rich combination of rock and sea, with extensive views over the Pyrenees and Cantabrian mountains, beautiful inlets for bathing, and shady, secluded nooks in which to read, smoke, or flirt. Biarritz has somewhat gone down since the Ex-Empress Eugenie retired into private life, but this no doubt will not detract from its merits in the eyes of many.

We secured seats on the top of the coach which leaves Biarritz for Bayonne, every half hour, and should have had a very pleasant drive, had we not been in mortal fear of losing an eye—or suffering some lesser calamity—from the driver's whip, which was some fifteen feet long; and, being flourished about in every direction, caused an incessant snapping, like the fire of musketry.

From Bayonne to the Spanish frontier, the pine becomes less common, being replaced by trees of various descriptions. Two pretty lakes are passed on the right; and fine views of the sea are also to be had, here and there, in the same direction. S. Jean-de-Luz is a quaint old town with a cathedral. From Hendaye, where the train stops, we walked along the road leading into Spain. The scenery is full of beauty and romance: on the right is seen the old Spanish town of Fuentearabia, celebrated by Milton.

Farther up the Bidassoa, and some short distance on the Spanish side, is Irun, at present besieged. We went as far as Behovie, a thriving-looking village. The frontier river, the Bidassoa, is here crossed by a bridge. On this side are the French soldiers; a few yards farther on, those of His Majesty, King Alfonso XII.; and the Spanish Behovia. How different the two villages!—that so peaceful—this bearing everywhere the impress of war: the church in ruins—the houses roofless and uninhabited—the marks of bullets in every direction. We heard that the Carlists were within twenty minutes' walk; but not wishing to come up with them, returned into France; and, ascending a small hill, took up a position commanding a magnificent panorama. Barring the desolated houses on the Spanish side, everything looked quiet enough, until a shell from a Carlist battery, aimed at the unhappy town of Irun, told us how illusory was this seeming tranquillity. We were now about three quarters of a mile from the latter place, and could distinctly hear the bugle calling the garrison to arms. Having heard the reports and seen the smoke of two more shells and some musketry, we returned to Bayonne; contemplating the sad picture of a country so beautiful, desolated by the ambition of contending princes.

CHAPTER II.

FROM BAYONNE TO VALLADOLID.

Santander — Custom-house Difficulties — Night Visitors — Music — "Our Brave Defenders" — Palencia — The Coro — Burgos Cathedral — Erratic Processions — The Fast Day — An Early Start — Arrival at Valladolid.

It was five o'clock on a Sunday morning when a small passenger steamer left the little town of Bayonne for the shores of Spain. Her captain and crew were Spanish, so were nearly all the passengers; we two being the only representatives of her Britannic Majesty's subjects.

About an hour after leaving Bayonne, we felt the waves of the Bay of Biscay heaving our little ship up and down; and soon lost sight of land, which did not reappear until about three in the afternoon. As we came in sight of the precipitous mountains which here form the coast of Spain, the wind, which had been freshening all the morning, blew half a gale, and had the effect of sending most of the passengers down-stairs, and of keeping us at sea two or three hours longer than we should otherwise have been.

Santander was reached about seven the same evening. There a motley crowd of at least a hundred persons—men, women, and children—had assembled to see the boat arrive. To anyone visiting Spain for the first time, the sight was truly a strange one. Two custom-house officials came on deck; but they said they had no power to examine the luggage. After some delay, we were allowed to take our small packages on shore; where we were guarded by two soldiers, who kept us prisoners for about half an hour, just as if we had been Carlists or brigands, instead of two harmless tourists. By this time it was dark, and we were allowed to transport what we had with us to the custom-house, where we were told that nothing could be examined that evening. By means of this arrangement, many of the passengers had the satisfaction of passing the night with nothing to console them but their umbrellas. As a great favour, a small carpet-bag which I had in my hand was accorded us, and we considered ourselves quite fortunate.

Santander was so full that we had to sleep in the dining-room of the hotel where we alighted. Several persons, of an inquiring turn of mind, came in to examine us at various hours of the night and early morning; most of them striking a match to facilitate their observations. However interesting this might have been to them it was anything but agreeable to us, who had just landed from a fourteen-hour sea-voyage, and sorely needed rest.

Santander is not a pleasant place for a lengthened stay—it has too much of the shipping and commercial element about it. It has a cathedral and a few churches; all of which might easily be mistaken, from their external appearance, for prisons or lunatic asylums. They rejoice in neither turret nor steeple; and the few small windows—or holes to admit light—are carefully barred with iron gratings. Internally they are gaudy; but, as a rule, devoid of artistic merit.

During our stay we had the honour and great felicity of harbouring in our hotel no less a personage than the Financial Minister of the Crown, with his wife and family. He did not seem to be much weighed down by the burden of his responsibility, nor the empty state of his exchequer; for he would sit down in the evening, and play the piano with a sort of *sans-souci* touch, which was quite charming to listen to.

Later on, music of a different kind would begin outside; three or four minstrels singing and playing in that lugubrious, monotonous style which is so common in all parts of Africa. There is an old saying, "Africa begins across the Pyrenees;" and when one hears the Spanish music, and sees some of the uninviting Spanish habits, one begins to perceive its force. The king was expected in Santander; but we were rather pleased when the news came that His Most Catholic Majesty had changed his mind—or somebody else had changed it for him: it would have sent prices, which were already rather high, up to a still more unwelcome figure.

At nine o'clock on the 10th of August, we proceeded on our journey south. The line, skirting the sea for a short way, affords some pleasant views of the hills across the bay which here indents the coast. At all the stations as far as Valladolid, some half dozen soldiers were drawn up in line on the arrival of each train. These "brave defenders," to judge from their youthful appearance, and the very irregular way in which they stood at "attention"—were for the most part raw recruits. What such a force would have done in the presence of even twenty or thirty of the enemy's veterans, it is not difficult to conjecture.

Luckily their services were not required, the days we travelled.

The country towards Reinosa, is, in parts, mountainous and grand. The engineering difficulties must have been great, as tunnel after tunnel occurs in rapid succession; the intervals between them affording fine mountain views. At Reinosa, we lunched; the meal consisting of soup, two kinds of meat —species unknown, a red vegetable—also unknown, fowl, biscuits, grapes, pears and peaches. Wine is always placed on the table, equally with water; and people help themselves *à discretion*.

Feeling somewhat refreshed, we re-entered our carriages; and continued ascending, until we reached an altitude of about 3,200 feet. On beginning the descent, we passed several flocks of sheep; but instead of their having the one traditional black sheep, which every orthodox flock is supposed to have, they seemed to have as many black as white—possibly typical of the Spanish nation. We saw some curious village churches, resembling barns in every respect; except that the western wall seemed to be built as high again as any of the others, and perforated in its upper part with oblong holes. Two Spanish officers, who had been discussing everything in general, and Carlists in particular, in such a loud tone of voice that it was evident they meant their comments for the benefit of the whole compartment, now turned their conversation upon religion; when one of them actually informed the other, that he believed in a God—rather a startling statement in this very Catholic country.

We now entered a wide desert plain, as flat as a pancake, and as uninteresting as the wilds of Sahara, except where a roofless house told of the ravages of war. We slept at Palencia—an uninteresting Spanish town; excepting perhaps for its cathedral, which is in the style of Leon, and its trees, which were quite pleasant after the barren track we had emerged from.

On going to the cathedral next morning,

we found its proportions sadly marred by the coro or choir. This obstruction exists in all Spanish cathedrals, and is placed in the centre of the middle aisle. It is formed by three walls from twelve to eighteen feet high, facing north, south, and west—generally well sculptured on the exterior, especially that which faces the principal entrance. The remaining side—the east—is shut in by an open screen; thus enabling the choir to see the altar, which is itself contained in a similar structure on a smaller scale, the only difference being that the open screen is on the west side. The space between this and the eastern part of the coro, is all that is practically available for the laity, and even this is generally curtailed by a passage up the centre, fenced with iron railings connecting the two. On each side of these railings assemble the faithful. As no chairs, or seats of any kind are provided, the women sit on the floor during the sermon and certain portions of the service; the men standing meanwhile. The coro is the most effectual manner yet invented of rendering a church thoroughly useless. It completely blocks up the view of the high altar from the greater part of the building; and has been unhappily somewhat imitated in England, as in the case of Westminster Abbey, and some of the other cathedrals which have not yet undergone restoration.

Two days of Palencia were quite enough; and we determined to leave for Burgos, the next morning, at 6.50; but owing to the circumstance of there being two stations— a fact which we have never forgiven our guide-book for not mentioning—we lost the train. As there was only one other—and that did not leave till late in the evening— we determined to return to our hotel and stay another day; thereby causing an immense amount of merriment to the employers and employed of that establishment. Profiting by this experience, we got ourselves fairly started the next morning, and arrived in that ancient capital—Burgos—about 10 a.m.

On emerging from the station, we came upon some thirty males of all sizes and ages, anxious to do anything and everything. Two or three of them tried to tear the small packages we carried out of our hands; others wished to drive us about the town in an omnibus; others again, wished to show us the way to the cathedral—quite unnecessary, as we were not likely to miss it. Such was the clamour and such the commotion to ascertain what hotel we were going to, and when we were going to see the town, that it was with the greatest difficulty we made our escape; notwithstanding my repeatedly telling them that we wanted nothing, and knew our own affairs better than they did. When in the city, we selected an hotel, and then sent for our luggage.

Perhaps the most beautiful building that Spain has ever produced, is the cathedral at Burgos. Words fail to give an adequate idea of this wonderful pile. Look where he will, the stranger cannot help being struck with the exquisite detail of every part. At the west end are two spires of the most delicate workmanship; each being of open fretwork, like the spire of Freiburg in Baden. Over the centre, is a magnificent lantern, in the shape of an octagon, rising nearly 200 feet from the pavement, and in some respects resembling that of Cologne. At the east end, is the Capilla del Condestable, the richest of the rich chapels which form so conspicuous a part of this edifice.

In the afternoon, we clambered up to an old castle lying on a hill outside and immediately above the town, said to have been standing some nine hundred years. It was as strongly guarded as if a Carlist surprise were expected to take place that evening.

The Cartuja di miraflores has a beautiful conventual chapel, which might at first sight be mistaken for a Greek church. Both this and Las Huelgas, which we subsequently inspected, are approached by shady avenues of trees, and lie from one to two miles outside the city walls. At

Las Huelgas, we were admitted into that part of the chapel which lies between the coro and the altar. The nuns were chanting vespers; and as we passed the open grating which enables them to see the celebrant, it was a great temptation to stop and peep at these saintly damsels.

This being the vigil of the Assumption, several small erratic processions went about the town, in the course of the afternoon. The first we saw, consisted of a priest, a boy, and a dozen gendarmes; another of five little boys dressed in red and white, one carrying a cross bigger than himself. At the corner of the square, the crucifer stopped for a few minutes; and two of the procession improved the occasion by turning into a pastrycook's hard by.

Great preparations were being made at the cathedral, for celebrating the coming festival with all due and appropriate rites. A large gilt canopy, the several pieces of which it took five men to carry, was erected over the high altar; and rich curtains were hung behind and around it. On the archiepiscopal throne was placed a life-sized figure of the Virgin, gorgeously dressed, and wearing a crown; before her, on a small table, were several vases of choice exotics, and two lighted tapers.

As this was a strict fast day, we were curious to see how the dinner went off at our hotel. At first we thought the fast was going to be scrupulously kept; for a great number of eggs were brought in, and speedily devoured by the Spaniards concerned. A bowl containing legs, wings, backs, etc., of chickens was placed before us, (non-fasters). When the eggs were finished, we were a little surprised to see one of the fasters take up our bowl; and, after having helped himself substantially, pass it on to his fellow-sinners, who all helped themselves in turn; as they did likewise to a dish of ham and potatoes, and another of mutton chops, which we at first thought had been prepared solely for our consumption. A plate of biscuits was now brought up for the fasters; of which, we, of course, did not partake. The usual courses of fruit finished the entertainment for all alike. From this we argued—" happy thought!"—next time fast day comes round, go in strongly for abstinence.

We were perpetually hearing about the Cid. We were expected to see the place where he was born—a bit of iron which he once used—nay more, if our guide was to be believed, we were expected to go into the town-hall, and see his bones! I don't approve of this habit of worrying the dead; so we saw none of them, and left the poor Cid to rest in peace.

The train we were destined to leave Burgos by, started at 5 a.m. Soon after 3 we heard a thumping at our door, and inquiries made as to whether we were ready. We certainly were not; and had no intention of being at that early hour. These attentions were continued at intervals of from five to ten minutes; and at last became so violent, that I had to get up and open the door, to know what was the matter. The omnibus, I was told, had been waiting for us so long, that it was doubtful whether it would wait any longer. We consequently got up; and after groping our way downstairs, were bundled into a springless concern drawn by two mules, which seemed in no particular hurry to start, after all. At length, we did proceed a short distance; and were then stopped by a gate. The driver got down, and wandered about the place, in order to find somebody who might have a key to this obstacle; but not being successful, he turned back, and drove to the station by another road, which appeared to have no gates *en route*. It is needless to say that we were there long before it was necessary; but this is what one is always subjected to in Spain.

The country about Burgos is a little more hilly than that we had lately been accustomed to. Soon after leaving Venta di Baños, the great junction of this line, it becomes barren in the extreme. We saw a building on the left, ugly enough to be a church ; and soon afterwards, on the right, a solitary tree, looking *in extremis;* and a few hundred yards further on, half a dozen more, much in the same plight—these were the approaches to Valladolid.

CHAPTER III.

AVILA AND THE ESCORIAL.

Valladolid — Feast of the Assumption—Auto-da-fés—the Alameda—Avila—Fever—Santa Teresa—Spanish Trains—the Escorial—the Panteon—Opening a Coffin—Relicario—Desolate Country—Madrid.

Our first work on arriving at Valladolid, was to clear ourselves of the miscellaneous crowd which always throngs the railway station of a Spanish town; our next, to visit the cathedral. This being the Feast of the Assumption of the B. V. M., more than the usual number of people had gathered in this unsightly and unfinished building. A straggling procession began the service; and after the gospel, a sermon was preached upon the excellence and high attributes of the mother of God. Some of the acolytes who happened to be near us, took this opportunity of dropping off to sleep, one of them snoring violently. The sermon ended, the Nicene creed was given with full orchestral accompaniment; and the service concluded about noon, having lasted two hours.

There is nothing to detain the stranger in Valladólid, unless he be of an historic turn of mind, and like to see the house where Philip II. was born, and that in which Columbus died; or the great square where the *auto-da-fés* were formerly given. Here the writhing Jew once shrieked for mercy, as the flames mounted around him— mercy denied by those who professed to be the servants of the Most Merciful. Here hundreds have died in the most excruciating agony, in order to satisfy that unforgiving and unrelenting monster which was,—surely by a stroke of the most consummate irony—designated " the *Holy Tribunal.*"

In the evening, we strolled along the Alameda (every Spanish town is provided with one of these promenades); and there we saw nearly the whole population disporting themselves by the glimmering of the pale moonlight. Dons and doñas were there by the score—soldiers and sailors—tinkers and tailors—ploughboys and thieves—everyone in fact; excepting perhaps the clergy, who, if there, had dropped their distinguishing dress for the occasion.

As we took the night train to Avila, we did not see much of the country; but concluded it was of the usual barren character—a conclusion which was confirmed by the glimpses we now and then caught.

At Avila, we found an hotel kept by an Englishman and his wife. These were the first compatriots we had spoken to, since leaving our native shores. Tourists who complain that they are continually meeting with their fellow-countrymen, wherever they go, should try this route; and I don't mind guaranteeing their comparative freedom—at any rate, as long as the war lasts. Our host told us he had not had more than a dozen English staying at his hotel this year; and as Avila is a place nearly everyone who comes to Spain makes a point of seeing, it shows how very scarce we must be. Here, I had a slight attack of fever, brought on by the excessive heat; and, for a whole day, subsisted on lemons and water. The fever, on departing, left an uncomfortable sore throat, which lasted for a fortnight.

. Avila cathedral, which, besides doing duty as such, forms a part of the fortifications, is a stern, massive building.

What is most thought of, however, is the shrine of Santa Teresa. This young lady, from a local account, was not one of those whose piety developed at a very early age; she did not refuse to play with her toys on Sunday, when only three years old, or decline to eat meat on Friday when only five. On the contrary, as she grew up she took a pleasure in the society of her friends, and even enjoyed frivolous amusements. However, being suddenly smitten with a sense of the vanity of all things here below, she determined to lead a "religious" life: but if woman is fair, woman is also fickle; and Santa Teresa, having changed her mind, again came forth into the world. Getting tired of this second turn of the flesh (it is lucky that women have a right to change their minds), she once more entered the convent, and it was now that her saintliness began. It was she who restored vigour and life to the laxity of the then existing religious houses; it was she who proclaimed the pains of purgatory to consist in the inability to love or be loved, and many other such things. I am aware that this version differs somewhat from the orthodox one, which declares that she thirsted for martyrdom at seven years old, etc., etc.; but if I have wronged Santa Teresa in any manner, I humbly beg her pardon.

We visited, during our stay, the now disused convent of San Tomas. This edifice contains the beautiful marble tomb of Don Juan, the hope of the Catholic kings, Ferdinand and Isabella, whose early death launched the crown into the hands of a foreigner. In the coro, which is in a west end gallery, instead of in the middle of the church, are the carved seats of Ferdinand and Isabella.

In this church is shown the spot where Santa Teresa, when one day communicating, had placed upon her, by the hands of angels, a white veil. It also contains a bust of Ferdinand *el Catolico*. This immense monastery, including the chapel, with all the ornaments and statues, was sold by the Government, at the time of its suppression in 1836. It was re-sold in 1859, for the ridiculously small sum of 15,000 dollars, (about £3,000,) the high altar, with its re-table and surrounding ornaments, being said to be alone worth that sum. Queen Isabella, who was the purchaser, handed it over to the Bishopric of Avila, in order that it might be preserved from secularization.

Curious old walls give quite a mediæval aspect to the town. It is some 3,500 feet above the sea, notwithstanding which, it seemed as hot as any of the places we had been in.

Notice the very convenient arrangement of Spanish trains. Three leave for Madrid, *per diem;* the first at 4.27 a.m., the second at 5.27 a.m., and the third in the afternoon. The second of these is styled by courtesy, an express, and has a peculiar privilege which is thoroughly continental; namely, that it does not take up passengers on this part of its journey, and only allows them to get out at about one station in six of those at which it stops. Although termed an express, and only carrying first-class passengers, it takes exactly the same time in performing the journey to Madrid as train number one, which takes up and puts down at all stations.

The railway, after leaving Avila, begins to ascend until it reaches an altitude of 4,500 feet, and then crosses an extensive plateau, very much resembling a Norwegian *fjeld.* Descending on the other side, we passed some pines, and, in due course, reached the Escorial, which lies surrounded by hills.

Ninety-nine persons out of every hundred who have read much, or thought much about the Escorial, would, I feel sure, on first seeing it, be egregiously disappointed. Viewed from the train, it looks like a magnified hotel, or bathing establishment, something similar to the Beau Rivage at Ouchy, or the National at Lucerne, except that it has a dome in its centre, and some smaller ones at its corners. This hotel-like aspect does not even disappear when more nearly approached. There are some trees leading up to it, quite pleasant to look upon in this treeless country.

On passing under the great gateway, one enters a large square called the Patio de los Reyes, although when we saw it, being filled with timber and other kinds of lumber, it did not look very regal. In front are six gigantic figures, each representing a Jewish king. I forgot to mention that over the gateway as we entered, is a life-size figure of S. Lawrence, in whose honour this immense pile was erected, and out of compliment to whom it was built in the shape of a gridiron.

From the west door, the whole beauty of the chapel is seen. It is large, with the dome for its centre, and an organ in each transept. The high altar is led up to by a long flight of rich red steps, which renders the service very effective. But the great gems, in my opinion, are the *ambones*—or two small pulpits—from which the epistle and gospel are occasionally read. These are exquisitely worked in different colours formed by jasper, porphyry, and marble, and surmounted by small gilt canopies. To the right and left of the altar, are kneeling figures of Charles V. and Philip II., besides several of their relations. Another great feature of this church is the absence of everything that is tawdry; there are no figures dressed in gauze, with paper crowns; all is solid and good—perhaps a little severe, but that is a fault in the right direction. Behind the altar, in the sacristy, is kept the miraculous wafer of Gorkum, which is said to have bled, in order to convince certain heretics as to the reality of sacramental doctrine. In the choir—which is in the same position as that of San Tomas at Avila—is the stall of Philip II.; and close by, the place where he was kneeling, when he first heard of the great naval victory of Lepanto.

We next descended into the Panteon, by a flight of marble steps. It is an octagonal building, placed immediately under the high altar; and contains the bodies of nine kings and eight queens, each in a marble coffin, on a shelf. The inscriptions are plain and simple: thus "Carolus III. Rex. Hisp." The coffin of Ferdinand VII. was first pointed out; and so regularly backwards; missing out Ferdinand VI. and Philip. V., who are buried elsewhere. As we neared the body of Philip II., I shuddered to think of the brain which had planned, and the hand which had signed, so many cruel, execrable orders. "At the foot of a mountain," said Philip, "with two inches of paper, I rule the world, both old and new." Yes! and ruled it in such a fashion as neither old nor new have yet forgotten! The present king of Spain was here last Maundy Thursday, to hear a mass for the repose of the souls of his ancestors. On that occasion, he caused the coffin of Charles V. to be opened. We were told by the sacristan that hardly any change could be perceived in the remains of that great emperor.

Leaving this chamber of death, and passing doors to the right and left, which led to the burial places of countless *Infantes* and *Infantas*, we again found ourselves in the church. In the cloisters, where Philip II. used to pace up and down, are numerous frescos of no great merit. After wandering about the building for some time, we looked through a hole in a door, and were a little surprised to find what the room contained: heads, legs, and arms were scattered in every direction, and in such reckless confusion as would have delighted the heart of any respectable surgeon. We afterwards learnt that this was a portion of the *relicario*, for which the Escorial is so famed. Philip II. was a great admirer of all relics; and it was he who laid the foundations of this gigantic collection. The following specimens are amongst the most famed—the bodies of San Mauricio and San Theodoro; those of many of the eleven thousand virgins, and of one of the Holy Innocents; a hand of Pope San Sixtus, a finger of San Lorenzo, and a bit of the gridiron on which he suffered.

As the rooms of the palace were being repaired, no one was allowed to see them. They comprise, among others, the one in which Philip II. lived; and a small one in which he died, at a good old age.

We took the evening train to Madrid; and passed over a country thickly strewn with fragments of rock, giving the scenery a very wild appearance. Then came a desolate table-land, one of the most barren tracts in Christendom. After a couple of hours, the lights of Madrid were visible; and presently we reached the station, and then our hotel.

CHAPTER IV.

MADRID AND TOLEDO.

Situation—Picture Gallery—Armoury—Men and Women—Fans and their uses—A Dusty Journey—Ancient Monuments of Toledo—Cathedral—Pugilistic Propensities—Beggars—Night Travelling—Andalucia at last.

MADRID, situated on a plain 2,500 feet above the sea, with a temperature varying from 16° to 104° Fahrenheit, and a rainfall averaging only $9\frac{1}{2}$ inches *per annum*, is the highest capital in Europe. It owes its creation to Philip II., who selected it as being the most central point in Spain. The court had hitherto been held at Valladolid; and far better would it have been had it remained there. Philip lived to recognize this, but it was then too late: new interests had sprung up, and what had been done must remain. So the capital enjoys its peculiarly privileged geographical position, at the expense of everything else. We found it to be a clean modern town, full of life and bustle. It has no cathedral or churches of any note; but has a wonderful picture gallery, said to be the finest in the world. Many of the pictures were brought from the Escorial; many came from England during the troubled times of the Commonwealth; and others from various parts too numerous to mention. The gallery is small when compared with that of Florence, but it contains pictures of which neither Florence nor Rome can boast.

The artists whose works we were most anxious to see, were Murillo, Velasquez, Zurbaran and Juanes. With the first of these, who could be disappointed? Nothing can be more exquisite than the softness of his female figures, and the expression which enlivens and vivifies every face. Richness of colour is among the chief of Juanes' many merits. With Velasquez, we were both disappointed. This might have been due to the uninteresting subjects he generally selects—portraits, or a man on horseback, or a friar begging, or some one person or thing; but if truth must be told, Velasquez we did not admire.

The *Armeria Real* of Madrid is to the other armouries of Europe what its *Museo* is to the picture galleries. The collection comprises almost everything used in medieval warfare. Many of the suits are ticketed as having been the property of Charles V. and subsequent kings. There are also some very interesting crowns and other regal insignia recently found near Toledo, belonging to sovereigns of a long buried dynasty.

All over Madrid, the Philips are continually cropping up; in front of the palace is a statue of Philip IV.—one of the things to be admired.

As the king was staying at the palace—I mean the live king, for we have been so much amongst dead kings lately that it is necessary to be explicit—we could not see the rooms; but had to content ourselves with looking at His Majesty's private chapel, where a service was going on. The organ is very superior to the generality of Spanish instruments, and occasionally delivered itself of very striking sounds.

The *Madrileños* did not wear the *capo*, or celebrated Spanish cloak, which covers the whole body, the end being thrown over the left shoulder. This may be due to two reasons; firstly, the exceptionally mild weather we had been enjoying—to-day the thermometer was 88° in the shade, rendering all great coats a little superfluous; and secondly, to a desire to imitate Parisian fashions—amongst which, the *capo* is not reckoned. The ladies wear no bonnets; but, instead, the black mantilla, which gives a very graceful appearance to their small-made figures. They are nearly all dark, with black eyes, and of prepossessing appearance; although hardly equalling their Italian sisters.

Every Spanish lady carries a fan, which she opens and shuts, on an average, several hundred times a day. A lady comes into church, kneels down; and, before she has remained in that position two minutes, has probably opened and shut her fan some twenty times. Or, she sits down to the dinner-table, opens her fan, fans herself for about three seconds, shuts it again, opens it the reverse way—and so on, until one would think the poor fan must give way under such incessant service.

Another use which these fans are put to, is that of conveying secrets. When a Spanish lady wishes to be very confidential, she places one end of the open fan to her mouth, and the other end to the ear of her confidant, in order that the sound may be conveyed straight to its destination, without rambling into ears for whose benefit it was never intended. It was in one of these fannish outbursts of confidence, that a young doña next to whom I had the felicity of sitting, informed me that she was a Protestant. I started, assuming the true Castilian whose nerves always receive a shock, when he hears that he is in sudden and close contact with a heretic. Upon my recovering myself sufficiently to ask her how long it was since she had forsaken the religion of her fathers, to take up with strange doctrines, she said about three years; and then went on to explain that at their chapel in Madrid, the pastor said two or three prayers, and then preached a sermon: the formulæ of Protestant worship seem to be much the same all over the world.

We also met with an Englishman who rejoiced in the knowledge of the fact that he was among the saved. He said he had been consoling himself with this reflection, for some years past; although, I regret to add, he was not equally sanguine about the condition of those around him—ourselves included. Before leaving, he read a portion of Scripture, and offered up a prayer; and so we parted the best of friends.

We got up early next morning, for we had to start for Toledo. The thermometer being now only 77°, it felt quite cool and pleasant. After having coffee at the station, we began the most unpleasant of railway journeys. The engine, as it traversed the plains of Castille, raised such a quantity of dust that, finding its way into the carriages, it nearly suffocated the passengers. We were glad to reach Aranjuez, where there are some trees and a palace. The next station, Castillejo, is the junction for Toledo. Sixteen miles more of uninteresting country brought us to what Murray grandiloquently describes as "the widowed capital of two dynasties."

As Madrid is the political, so Toledo is the ecclesiastical metropolis; being the seat of the Primate, who in former times exercised great influence over the destinies of the country. It abounds in churches; indeed, in some instances, they are so close that one wall seems to do duty for two churches, just as in a row of houses. The ecclesiologist must not, however, think that he has unlimited interest before him, as ninetenths of them are not worth seeing; and the remaining tenth interesting mostly on account of their extreme old age, or from having once been a mosque, temple, or synagogue. El Christo de la Vega, a little unpretentious-looking building outside the walls, was converted into a church twelve hundred and fifty years ago; having previously been a heathen temple. El Christo de la Luz, once a mosque, is another of this type. The names of both testify to their great antiquity; for had they been christened in the twelfth or thirteenth century, they would have been certainly called Santa Maria de la *this*, or Santa Maria de la *that;* as indeed are the two synagogues which were converted into churches about the time above mentioned.

Toledo derives a certain amount of picturesqueness from being situated on esven mounds, and having the river Tagus flowing half way round it. With regard to vegetation, it is as destitute as the rest of the country, except just on the banks of the river. The streets are narrow, and almost devoid of vehicles. It retains much of its Moorish aspect, being but little altered, notwithstanding its eight hundred consecutive years of Christian rule.

Its cathedral is by no means the finest in Spain, although perhaps the most interesting. The Mozarabic chapel is at the south-west extremity; in it is daily celebrated mass after the ancient Mozarabic rite, which differs considerably from the Roman, and was universal in Spain till the end of the eleventh century, when the ascendency of Rome caused its suppression in favour of the Latin use. Round the high altar of the cathedral are buried some of the earlier kings of Spain. Here we find that there were other people in the world— and even kings—besides Philips II., III., and IV., of whom we have been hearing so incessantly in Madrid and the Escorial. The Capilla de los Reyes Nueves contains the bodies of monarchs of a later date, although anterior to the Philips.

On Sunday morning, after high mass, as

the acolytes were leaving their places in the coro, one pushed the other on to the floor; upon this he, getting up, endeavoured to kick the offender, who in his turn endeavoured to kick him. No doubt acolytes, like other boys, ought to be allowed to settle their little differences in their own way; but there is a time and a place for all things, and we, with our English ideas, might reasonably be excused for thinking the church hardly a fit place—nor immediately after divine service a fit time—nor red cassocks and white surplices a fit costume —in which publicly to display pugilistic propensities. However, every country has its own ways. After leaving the cathedral, we entered Santa Maria la Blanca, one of the synagogue churches referred to. It is to be feared that these did not fall into Christian hands by very fair means, but perhaps one had better not inquire too closely.

The celebrated Toledo blade and ammunition manufactory is situated on the Tagus, a mile from the town, and is worked entirely by water power. Here we saw bullets in all stages of manufacture; perhaps the very identical ones which will, in due course, stick in some Cuban or Carlist. Here also were swords for the cavalry; swords which had been proved, and swords which had not been proved; swords which would bend double, and swords which would not bend at all. Feeling quite military, we left this manufacture of death, and returned to Toledo.

There is a strange place here, called the Cave of Hercules. No one seemed exactly to know its whereabouts. By way of finding it out, as nearly as possible, I asked one of the priests—who are generally the most enlightened people in the town. He said its entrance was not known, and that it would be profanation to enter it even if it were. Some strange legends are connected with this cave; one is that Roderick, the last of the Goths, lost his kingdom by entering it.

The beggar is a noticeable feature in all

Spanish towns. They would be incomplete without him; just as an Italian picture would be without the conventional blue sky. He is not necessarily in want of money, nor is it to be taken for granted that he is lame or blind because he affects these disorders. Begging is a trade, and as such, very often has to counterfeit what it does not possess. Any lady or gentleman not being blessed with an income—or whose income is inadequate to his or her requirements—takes to begging as a cheap, speedy, and safe means of raising the wind; and its peculiar advantage, in the eyes of many, is that it entails but little trouble. The Church has always encouraged giving to beggars, and so it is that they thrive. The Government, having an eye to every means of raising the deplorable financial condition of the country, makes capital out of them, by compelling each to take out a license before letting him follow his profession. When this is done he is allowed to annoy the public to the extent he thinks proper; a privilege he never fails to exercise whenever he finds any unhappy member of the community tied to any particular spot—as when a traveller happens to be waiting to take his ticket at a railway station, or looking after his luggage: it is then that the beggar has him in his power, and seldom desists from his importunities until he has extracted a donation.

Every parish has a certain number of these miscreants on its roll, who are generally to be found in the morning sitting outside the church door, mumbling and grumbling whenever anyone passes. No one need fear ruining himself by indulging them to a small extent—a farthing or a halfpenny is considered handsome, and a penny princely. Should you, however, feel indisposed to give, you must not, as in England, say, "I have nothing for you," or "I shall give you in charge." Spanish politeness forbid! The true Castilian answer is, " My brother (or my sister), everything that I have is yours; but this time, for the love of God, you will pardon my not giving." Some such reply, next to a donation, is the most effectual manner of dealing with them; and I recommend it to everybody whom pleasure or business brings into the Peninsula. A good many of the hotels have a beggar attached to them; it is not at all uncommon to find one of this species, and a bootmaker, at the entrance to second-class inns. In conclusion, the Spanish beggar has nothing attractive about him whatsoever; he wears no picturesque costume, dresses in no bright colours, and is generally filthy. It is to be hoped that some day an enlightened Government (if Spain ever possesses such a thing) will find out some means of dispensing with this fry altogether; to the suppression of indolence and deception on the one hand, and of indiscriminate charity on the other—charity which always does more harm than it ever did good.

To the south of Toledo, lies a long uninteresting piece of country, in many places the scene of Don Quixote's adventures. Travellers generally go from here straight to Cordova, a distance, by rail, of two hundred and fifty miles. Two trains daily—notice their arrangement. The first leaves Toledo at seven in the morning, and gets to Cordova at two o'clock the next morning—a nice, convenient, pleasant time for arriving in a strange place. The other leaves at six in the evening, and reaches Cordova at 12.41 the next day. This looks a little better; but the traveller must not delude himself with the belief that it has no disadvantages;—four hours and a half of the night have to be spent at the wretched junction of Castillejo, with nothing but a board to lie upon, coarse bread and dried fish to eat, and the common red wine of the country to drink. After enduring this penance, and preferring to take nothing rather than the proffered viands, we were allowed to proceed to Alcazar, where there is a capital restaurant, and the train makes a halt of half an hour, in order that travellers may refresh themselves.

At Manzanares is the junction for Portugal. Two trains were drawn up; the one on the right side of the platform, the other on the left. If you wished to go to Andalucia, you stepped in on the left side; if to Portugal, on the right. But as this was rather an important step, before the trains started, the guard came round to every carriage, to ascertain if passengers' tickets corresponded with their tastes. It now began to get light; and about 5 a.m. we passed through a small chain of mountains, and soon afterwards entered Andalucia. This province is supposed to be the garden of Spain; it has always been the theme of both poets and prose writers, and is generally over-rated by those who know nothing about it. It is fertile when compared with the rest of Spain; but this is not saying very much. The aloe and the Barbary fig flourish on their own account; but almost everything else has to be brought, planted, and watered;—*then* it will luxuriate. As the day advanced, the heat became intense—hotter, if possible, than it had been at Madrid and Toledo; and by the time we got to Cordova, it was almost insupportable.

CHAPTER V.

CORDOVA AND SEVILLE.

The Mosque and its Dignitaries—Marvel of Andalucia—Exposing the Dead—Cathedral—Murillos—Giralda—Alcazar—Inquisition—Judas Iscariot—Ground-floor rooms.

THE world-renowned Mosque of Cordova—now the cathedral,—is a quadrilateral building surrounded by a wall about 40 feet high, 600 feet long, and 450 feet broad. The cathedral proper occupies rather more than half the enclosure; the remaining portion being the Court of Oranges, an open oblong which, besides the trees from which it derives its name, contains two large palms, the first we had seen on our journey south—and perhaps the identical ones planted by the celebrated Abderahman himself. Standing at the entrance of the church, the *coup d'œil* is marvellous—magnificent—transcending all description. Look where you will—pillars, pillars, pillars. After recovering from our astonishment, the first thought that struck us was, "What must be the acreage of the edifice?"—I was going to say *square mileage*, but object to exaggeration. Stay! a large high protuberance in the very centre of the building catches the eye; what can this be? We go to examine it—good heavens! a coro. Yes; there was the veritable Spanish coro, with its three walls, marring the beautiful structure, just as a large black smudge in the centre would mar a Titian or a Raphael. Alas for Spanish taste! On inquiring who was the perpetrator of this enormity, we found it was a bishop of the sixteenth century who, aided and abetted by the dean and chapter, caused to be erected the coro. I rather imagine the reason for it was this: canons minor canons, prebendaries, etc., do not like being in public; a certain sense of shame then prevents them from cracking their little jokes during the service, or dropping off to sleep during the sermon; so, to avoid observation, they surround themselves with three high walls, and are thus unseen of all save their fellow-sinners—as any one on the open side would naturally be looking towards the altar, and not at them.

But to return to the cathedral. It occupies between three and four acres of ground, and contains upwards of a thousand marble or precious stone pillars, rising directly from the floor; instead of being placed, as is usually the case, upon some stone pedestal, about three feet high. According to tradition, no two are exactly the same length: this signified to the Moors, the different sects into which the Christian religion was split up.

The houses in Cordova are very pretty, with their little square *patios*, white marble pillars, and clean tesselated floors; a fountain in the centre, surrounded by oleanders, figs, and bananas, giving them a cool inviting appearance during the hot summer months.

We did not stay more than a day; but during that time, suffered much from the hotel beggar, who, taking up a commanding position just outside our door, jabbered at us in a most dictatorial manner. I am surprised that such a respectable hotel should keep a beggar to bully the visitors; and were I the proprietor of a Spanish inn, I should certainly put at the end of my advertisement, " No beggar kept."

We left for Seville at two in the afternoon. In this part of Spain the aloe is very abundant, and is used for hedges; a capital fence too, as bold would be the man, and bolder the quadruped, who tried to force a passage through these prickly obstacles.

Seville is one of those fortunate places which does not lack for trumpeters. Many persons rave about it. When any one hears that anyone else has been in Spain, the first question is, " Have you been in Seville? Have you seen Seville cathedral?" The Spaniards follow in the same strain.

"Who has not seen Seville," say they, "has not seen a marvel." So naturally as we neared this marvel of Andalucia, our expectations became a little high. And now for this eighth wonder of the world, as it appeared to us. A large town built in the Moorish style, on the left bank of the Guadalquiver, which here runs through a plain singularly devoid of the picturesque. Art has, however, in some measure supplied to Seville the attractions which nature has denied. Let us take her charms *seriatim*, lest we be dazzled by their brilliancy if we attempt to look at them *en masse*.

Firstly, the cathedral—said to come next to S. Peter's in point of size. On approaching it from the south, my attention was arrested by what looked like a small chapel in the wall, before which the passers-by raised their hats. Coming nearer, we found we were not mistaken; there was the black altar, crucifix, and lighted candles; and immediately in front, an open coffin, in which lay the body of a woman. Whether this soul was torn from the body in racking pain, or whether it softly went its way, like an angel's tread; whether she who now lies here, walked humbly with her God, or followed the paths of sin—it is not for us to inquire. "May she rest in peace," can but be the prayer of every Christian, as he passes by the remains of one who has gone before. A strange custom this of displaying the dead to public gaze; but it may help to recall the living to the shortness of our present existence, and the uncertainty of human life.

In the cathedral, no one can help being struck with its size and grandeur, as well as the admirable way in which it is proportioned; but when this has been said, it is about all. It is entirely devoid of that richness of detail which is the great feature at Burgos. The west front is poor in the extreme; and the pillars are without a single figure or adornment of any kind. All that Spaniards could do to mar the proportions of the building, they have done.

High metal gratings rail off the side chapels, giving them the appearance of dens for wild beasts, rather than Christian places of worship. The enclosure containing the high altar, has, besides the usual ones, a second smaller set, about a yard in front; as if, being intended for animals of a still more dangerous and ferocious character, it had been necessary to prevent visitors from approaching too near the bars. What would be the Lady Chapel elsewhere, is here called the Capilla di San Ferdinando; and contains, beside the remains of that warlike saint, his sword and banner. It was he who took Seville and Cordova from the Moors, in the thirteenth century; and for these acts he was sainted in due course; just as in England, he would have been knighted. Several semi-military, semi-ecclesiastical performances take place in his chapel every year, and are no doubt largely attended—by the fair sex.

This cathedral possesses its share of pictures, some being Murillos. Of their merits I cannot speak, as they are so placed that, without the eyes of a lynx, it is impossible to see them. Those in the Picture Gallery are naturally seen to greater advantage. Santa Justina and Santa Rufina protecting the Giralda, most took my fancy. These ladies are the patronesses of Seville, and are consequently held in high local repute. Every province of Spain has its saints, who, although much esteemed in their own districts, are very often but slightingly spoken of in other parts of the Peninsula.

The Giralda, which the saints above referred to are supposed to take so much care of, is the ancient Moorish tower. It is altogether 350 feet high, and contains the bells. In Italy it would have been called a fine *campanile*, and little more said about it. Here, it is considered almost sacred. The Moors certainly held it in very high veneration; and the Sevillians follow in their footsteps. To ascend it there are no stairs, but thirty-four gradual slopes, similar to those at S. Mark's at Venice, each being the length of one of the sides of the tower. From the summit a fair view is to be had of the cathedral, the town, the river, and the flat country. Nervous people should be careful that the big bell does not start off when they are up there, or the shock might make them jump over the parapet.

The Alcazar—I may here mention, for the benefit of those who do not know Arabic, that Alcazar means in that language " the palace "—is in the Alhambra style, although rather inferior, and consists of a beautiful *patio*, and rooms whose walls and ceilings are quite works of art. Anyone wishing to get a good idea of these buildings, and not caring to travel quite so far as Seville or Granada, has only to visit the Alhambra Court at the Crystal Palace, and imagine a number of additional rooms. Although very cool and airy in summer, this palace must be rather draughty in winter, as it has no doors, an open arch giving access from one room to another. The absence of furniture also adds to the uninhabitable appearance.

Behind are gardens and some peculiar fountains. One of them, which was turned on for our benefit, issued in numberless small jets from two cross paths, thereby itself making a cross. Palms and other tropical trees adorn this garden; also a tank where one of the kings—I think Philip V.—used to fish. We were shown some baths underneath the palace, and at the further extremity one or two dungeons.

Dungeons and Seville combined, put me in mind of the Inquisition, which had here one of its chief centres of operation. A small church is shown in the Alameda, where it is said the members held their last sitting, somewhere about 1808. Burnings used to go on at the close of the eighteenth century, but I am not aware whether the nineteenth has been disgraced by any such exhibitions.

Perhaps nowhere in the whole world has Christianity been presented to mankind in a worse form than in Spain and the Spanish dependencies. The greatest crimes which the heart of man can conceive, the greatest cruelty and torture which one human being can inflict upon another, have here been practised and gloried in, under the sacred name, and under the sacred seal of the religion of Christ. For a verification of this, we need look no farther than the records of the so-called Holy Office, the "Acts to suppress Heresy," enforced by the Duke of Alva in the Netherlands, and the atrocities committed in Mexico and Peru.

The results of forcing Christianity down the throats of the people, "whether they would hear, or whether they would forbear," are now only too apparent in the infidelity which is fast spreading over the Peninsula. The system of persecution so long pursued, never did more than gain for the Church a semblance of uniformity, at the expense of every one of her fundamental doctrines; and many a Spaniard has cursed from his heart of hearts that to which he may just have been showing all outward tokens of respect and submission.

The irreverence of the clergy in the present day also helps to lower religion in the eyes of the masses. The services are performed in a perfunctory manner, and the ceremonial gone through with an indecorous haste. In the cathedral at Malaga, I have seen high mass, with all its many accessories, celebrated in twenty-eight minutes. The genuflections are frequently omitted by the assistant clergy; and the elevation is often so slight that it is doubtful whether it would even come under the condemnation of the Judicial Committee of the Privy Council. The chasuble resembles the Italian in shape, but is generally rather longer, with one straight line of embroidery down the back. These vestments have no cross behind, either in Spain or Italy. The Sunday I spent at Toledo, two altar-lights only were used in the cathedral at high mass, and indeed it is rare for the number to exceed four, except upon very special occasions.

Seville still goes in for bull-fights, to a great extent. The ring is one of the finest in Spain; and the bulls slaughtered are of an exceptionally good breed. Respect for the resurrection of our Lord is shown by the best performances taking place on Sunday, Monday, and Tuesday in Eastertide. The week before this, religious ceremonies follow one another almost incessantly. A dance takes place before the high altar; this is peculiar to Seville. The Host is exhibited on the Monumento on Thursday.

On Holy Saturday vengeance is meted out to Judas Iscariot. Figures of him are hung about the town, generally filled with gunpowder, or some such explosive substance. Those who prefer to assist in blowing up Judas, rather than at the mass, take up a position in front of the apostle, having previously provided themselves with guns. When the church bells are rung to announce that the singing of the *Gloria in Excelsis* has commenced, they blaze away until Judas goes off with a pop.

Others prefer to take him down, and beat him; others to throw stones at him; in short, every Christian feels it his bounden duty to inflict some injury on the Son of Perdition. There are also many other minor rites practised in the Holy Week, which here pass under the name of religion.

The curious little church of Santa Maria la Blanca—like that at Toledo—was once a Jewish synagogue. In the celebrated tobacco manufactory, are employed five thousand women and girls, making cigars and cigarettes—so great is the demand for these soothing narcotics.

Seville was the hottest place we had been in. . The thermometer could not be induced to go below 90°, notwithstanding the many appliances for keeping the houses cool; and when the wind came down the narrow *calles*, or streets, it was like a blast from a furnace. We were advised to get rooms on the ground-floor, as the difference of temperature between those so situated and those upstairs is very considerable.

Our windows, which were duly barred with strong iron gratings, looked on to a narrow but crowded street. It was impossible to close either windows or shutters, on account of the heat; so we were on view the whole time, and felt like two wild animals being exhibited. Everyone who chose, came to have a good look; and a splendid vantage ground it afforded the beggars, who could gather round our gratings, and mumble away by the half hour. How we longed for the double set of railings with which the high altar of the cathedral is provided! It was bad enough to be thus bearded in our den during the day, but a far worse trouble awaited us during the night. Unfortunately, we had not noticed the want of mosquito curtains; so as soon as our human tormentors had left, the mosquitos would begin their buzzing and biting, until relieved by the morning beggar. The day at last came for our departure; and 6 p.m., on the 5th of September, saw us in the train for Cadiz.

CHAPTER VI.

CADIZ AND GIBRALTAR.

Old Coins—A Bishop's Sermon—Change of Plans—Trafalgar—No Pier—Gibraltar—Galleries—Stalactite Caves—Monkeys—Military Funeral—All Alone.

For the first few miles of our journey, the country was very fertile; but this did not last long; it soon became thoroughly Spanish. Night closing in prevented our seeing more. On getting out at one of the small stations, to buy a glass of water, I received as change a copper coin of Ferdinand and Isabella. This must have been in circulation some three hundred and fifty years; and was, nevertheless, a good impression. Silver coins of the early part of the last century are very common, and some remarkably clear; but I never saw a copper one so old as this. It is said that in some of the small villages of the Castilles, coins of Philip II. are not at all rare; but I cannot vouch for the accuracy of the statement.

Cadiz was hot—insufferably hot compared with any weather we have in England; but oh! what a difference between it and Seville. The sea breezes in the early morning,before the sun was up, and in the evening after he had set, were like new life to us who had just come from the centre of Spain. Being built at the extremity of an island, it has the sea on three sides; and its foundation is said to be as old as the Patriarchs, though it does not look as ancient as Seville, Cordova, or Toledo. It has a nice Alameda, or promenade; and is well lighted, and comparatively clean.

There are two cathedrals, an old one and a new one; the latter being the finer. A notice was placarded on the doors, that on the 8th, the nativity of the B. V. M., a sermon would be preached by the bishop.

It is rather a rare thing in Spain for a bishop to preach; so, on the day in question, the cathedral was for once crowded. High mass began at nine; and after the chanting of the gospel, the right reverend gentleman ascended the pulpit. His sermon was a masterly oration, in defence of the seven festivals of the B. V. M. Each was dealt with singly, and then they were considered generally. The arguments that heretics and infidels of all shades had dared to use in disparagement of these high occasions were next dealt with. The bishop would now mercilessly knock to pieces the arguments of some unhappy Protestant whom he had singled out. His lordship would then set up imaginary ones of his own, which some future heretic might use, in order to fell them to the ground with a blow. Every now and then, when quite exhausted, he would sit down for two or three minutes, in order to take breath, wipe his head, and perform that nasty operation of spitting, which is common to all Spanish clergymen, whether bishops, priests, or deacons; then, clearing his throat and drinking a little water, he would return to the charge like a giant refreshed. When this had gone on for a couple of hours, two members of the chapter left their seats in the coro, and proceeded to the pulpit; one of them ascended, and whispered something to the bishop. Although I did not hear, I conclude it was to the effect that, while not wishing in any way to hurry his lordship, still if he could manage to bring his remarks to a close in the course of the afternoon it might be as well—for a few minutes after the sermon ended. As in England, so in Spain, the preaching over, crowds of people left the church, and the holy mysteries were then celebrated for the benefit of those who remained. In the afternoon there was a procession, consisting of the bishop and his clergy, naval officers in full uniform, and ladies and gentlemen in evening dress.

We were to have gone to Lisbon, but on inquiring at the office, were told that the steamer would not touch there. I rather fancy that ships arriving from Spanish ports were put into quarantine; we had for some time past had our doubts as to these places being as healthy as they might be. It was no good regretting Lisbon; there was nothing to be done but go to Gibraltar. So, on the 10th, we embarked for that destination. A high sea was running at the time, and the habit, so universal in Spain, of embarking and disembarking in small boats, is by no means unattended with danger on these occasions.

As we rounded the promontory, the waves tossed the little vessel about to such an extent that it became quite alarming. Luckily the sea, instead of increasing, moderated as the day went on; or the papers might have had to record "Foundering of a Spanish steamer at sea—all hands," etc. Half way between Cadiz and Gibraltar lies Cape Trafalgar, a rocky-looking headland, ending in a lighthouse. Here England's victory was sealed by the death of one of her bravest heroes. Tarifa—sometimes said to be the southernmost point in Europe (though I believe Cape Matapan, in Greece, to be farther to the south)—is another promontory resembling Trafalgar, and also ending in a lighthouse.

The Moorish coast is here distinctly visible; and it is said that between this point and Gibraltar a change in the colour of the sea can be perceived, marking the meeting of the Atlantic and Mediterranean. We now entered the Bay of Gibraltar, and touched at Algeciras, a small Spanish town on the western shore. Having disembarked a few Spaniards, we steamed across and dropped anchor.

One would have thought that, Gibraltar being under English rule, a pier would have been built, and the necessity of small boats dispensed with. But not at all; we were as badly off in this respect as in the most uncivilized parts of Spain, and were told, to boot, that a pier would make the fortress too accessible. I suppose the British Lion is afraid that an enemy might quietly land his men here, whilst he was asleep.

One's first impression of Gibraltar is that it is over-crowded; there seems not to be enough room for the numbers of people who congregate there, and the authorities do not like the accommodation to be increased —no doubt for the same excellent reason that is given for the non-construction of a pier. Every nationality and creed is represented at Gibraltar: Jews, Turks, infidels and heretics live and luxuriate in perfect harmony, under the benign influence of the British rule. Here may be seen the turbaned Moor, the Barbary Jew, the Italian and the Greek, the African negro and the heathen Chinee—a cosmopolitan place indeed. The inhabitants of the town are however principally Spanish.

Of course the fortifications are the great thing in Gibraltar. Permission to view them must be obtained from the military secretary. Pieces of light artillery, weighing several hundred tons, more or less, lie scattered about in every direction. The newest are muzzle-loaders; the breech-loading system for artillery having been found to be a mistake. The galleries excavated in the rock contain each its own complement of guns, ready to do terrible execution on any enemy bold enough to approach them; the gunners incurring hardly any risk. To silence one of these batteries would be next to impossible, considering that the small apertures through which the guns discharge their contents are the only places where a hostile fire could do any mischief.

The most curious natural phenomena of which the rock boasts, are however the stalactite caves. I visited them in company with a friend very well known in Gibraltar, and consequently had no need of a permission, now rather difficult to obtain, on account of accidents which have taken place there. We started at 10 a.m., and met, according to appointment, a sergeant of

artillery and six privates at the entrance.
Each being armed with a lighted candle,
we began the descent on the left. Stooping was always necessary; but here and
there the rocks were so low overhead that
crawling had to be resorted to. A few
minutes brought us into a good sized cave.
I had little idea, before we entered, of the
great beauty of stalactites; at one side they
resembled the columns of a church; and
others had the appearance of icicles. As
we groped our way about these hidden
recesses of the earth, our candles but
making darkness visible, a sort of mysterious awe unconsciously crept over me.
More crawling, of a still more abject
character, through crevices hardly two
feet in any direction, brought us to a yet
finer cave. We had now gone as far as
we could in that direction; so, returning
to the place from whence we started, began
to explore the right side. There is a black-looking hole, into which we threw stones,
and listened till—in the far distance—we

could hear them striking the rocks, as they hurried through space. Our sergeant informed us that this was called the Bottomless Pit, and that no one had ever been down it, except one officer, who never came back; but I subsequently learned that this was not the case, as a gentleman whom I met on the rock told me that he had been down it himself, in company with a lieutenant of artillery; adding that they let themselves down by knotted ropes, and found great difficulty in getting up again.

We bade adieu to the caves; and, in returning to Gibraltar, saw several of the celebrated monkeys, the only wild ones in Europe. They are now twenty-three in number, and it is considered the next thing to sacrilege to molest them.

I had hardly laid my pen down, this afternoon, when the strains of the band were heard in the distance—not in its usual lively style, but slow and mournful. At first I failed to recognise the "Dead March in Saul"; but the reversed muskets of the advanced guard, the slow steady march, and, last of all, the coffin, all proclaimed the solemn procession of the dead. The cemetery lies just outside the town, with the rock rising abruptly on one side of it, looking like a grim sentry guarding its charge. Thither the mournful *cortège* bent its way. The few prayers over, the body lowered, the salute was fired. The old rock echoed it back: an English soldier had gone to his rest.

At Gibraltar I parted from my brother, who returned to England by the P. & O. boat, and continued my journeyings alone.

CHAPTER VII.

TANGIER.

Civilization and Barbarism—Landing—Deserted Streets—
the Soko—Camels—Weddings and Funerals—Fez Etiquette—Slavery—Departure.

THE favourite excursion from Gibraltar, is to the Moorish city of Tangier, distant some twenty-eight miles across the Straits, in a south-westerly direction. These two towns, owing to their close proximity, are in frequent communication. Indeed, except in bad weather, the rock is distinctly visible from Tangier. Notwithstanding this, their general aspect is so different, that it is difficult to believe that they are not a thousand miles apart. Nowhere can such a complete contrast be met with, in so short an interval of space. Nowhere do civilization and barbarism so nearly approach. The one has been already described: English laws, English justice; its head a constitutional sovereign. The other is ruled by an African autocrat, the most unapproachable of Barbary princes; whose changeable will is his country's only law, and in whose sound judgment is his country's only hope.

I will now describe a visit which I made to Tangier in the winter of 1872. The traveller who goes there to-day will find but little change, as Eastern habits are slow to vary.

The steamer takes four hours in crossing; and as she neared the African coast, a number of boats filled with half-dressed Arabs could be perceived, making for her, under full oar. They soon came up, swarming like vultures round a carcase, and yelling and shrieking like jackals eager for their prey. My portmanteau was the occasion of a brisk little skirmish between the proprietors and abettors of the different boats.

It fell, but happily did not fall into the sea; a savage had secured it, and as he did so, raised a fiendish cry of triumph. Where my luggage went, I was obliged to follow. And now I thought our troubles were over until we reached *terra firma;* but getting within a few yards of the shore, some natives with bare legs ran into the water. One of them—a horrid-looking nigger— endeavoured to pick me up bodily; there was nothing to be done but to cling to him, and so I was landed.

Some others were destined for the same hotel as myself; and as we went up the silent, narrow streets, occasionally meeting a pallid ghost-like figure dressed in white, it seemed like what one reads of the cities of the departed, more than anything I can compare it to. No cracking of whips—no bustling to and fro, to mar the silent harmony. All was still, even to a mysterious stillness; the sun had just set, and the inhabitants, for the most part, had retired to their houses.

At the entrance of the hotel, we saw an Arab, fully six feet high, standing erect in his Eastern dress, with turbaned head. I looked at him with profound reverence—a reverence which his stately and majestic bearing justly called forth.

"This must be some great Arab chief," I thought to myself—"the leader of a noble band," when, to my utter astonishment, I heard the English language issuing from his venerable mouth.

"I am Mahomed," he said, "the guide of the hotel; I shall be very happy to take you round, and show you the sights."

"Thank you," I replied, feeling a little taken aback, as well as taken down. "When do we dine?"

"At half-past six."

"All right."

The next morning, the principal street was by no means so deserted as my first impressions had led me to expect. Indeed, just outside one of the gates, the soko—or market-place—where a fair was being held, presented quite a lively scene. The principal vendors were women; each being squatted down by the side of her property, and waiting for customers, scales in hand. The chief articles sold are bread, meal, vegetables, butter, milk, goat-skins, and earthenware utensils; in fact, everything which an Arab household could reasonably require was to be picked up here at moderate prices. As I looked round upon the strange scene, and listened to the Babel of voices which rose about me, my eyes lighted upon some camels, and I began to wonder if the patience of Job could ever have exceeded the patience of these animals. They looked put upon, poor things; and how they ever survive the days and days of travelling in the scorching desert, with little food and no water, it is difficult to imagine.

One day, when returning from a walk along the piece of sandy beach which stretches in a south-easterly direction from the town, I heard the rapid discharge of musketry within the walls. Could this be an *émeute?*

Had the tyranny of the Government become such that no one could any longer stand it? This might be the commencement of the glorious republic of Morocco; and if I only hurried, I might be a privileged spectator! I entered, all enthusiasm to know who were the victors.

It was only a wedding!

Half-a-dozen lunatics, with the usual flint and steel Moorish guns, about seven feet long, were in the wildest state of excitement, heading the procession; running about, throwing up their arms, and blazing away as fast as they could reload; then the music, which, if once heard, can never be forgotten; next the bride, inside a box placed on the back of a mule—and consequently invisible to the bystanders; then the bridegroom, riding his mule, and accompanied by his friends; and finally a miscellaneous crowd of admiring children, who always follow anything attended with noise. This procession goes about the streets for several hours, and eventually deposits the bride at her husband's house. In honour of such an event, beating of drums, and other means for producing disagreeable sounds, are generally resorted to during the whole night, pleasantly reminding the weary tourist that he is in a barbarous country, and that sleep and morning may be expected together.

For a funeral, as well as for a marriage, noise is the great point aimed at. When a decease occurs, the proper thing is to secure the services of half-a-dozen of the ugliest and most loathsome niggers in the town. Each comes with some instrument of music; and, having formed a circle, they play and sing by the hour, swaying their bodies backwards and forwards, and turning themselves round. One will occasionally, as if by a kind of inspiration, rush into the middle of the ring, and there perform a set of private evolutions; having by this means, I suppose, let off some of his superfluous feelings, he will return to his post. This performance may continue for hours, days, or weeks, according to the respect in which the deceased was held, and the ability of his relations to pay for the same. The actual ceremony of interment, as I saw on one occasion, consists of placing the body on a board, covering it over with linen, and burying it in the cemetery outside the town.

There are several mosques in Tangier, besides a number of saints' tombs, which, amongst other uses, afford sanctuary to criminals. The position which women occupy in regard to things sacred, may be gathered from the following saying:—" Let not a woman or a dog call the faithful to prayers." So, five times a day, a man ascends to the minarets; and after informing the passers-by, in a loud tone of voice, that " God is great, God is great," etc., he adds, " Come to prayers, come to prayers;" and, to his morning call, " Prayer is better than sleep." Tangier is generally honoured by the presence of a man whose sanctity extends to the limits of the Mahomedan world, he being the direct lineal descendant of the Prophet, and so ranking as first Shreef. His name has rather come before the British public of late, on account of his having taken to himself an English wife. He receives general adulation and homage wherever he goes, and has the privilege of having his hand kissed by the Sultan.

The etiquette at the court at Fez is somewhat singular, as it is never permitted to use the word "death" in the presence of the sovereign : " Mr. A. has gone to sleep," or " Mrs. B. has been called away." If it is necessary to introduce a Jew or Christian, some such remark as the following has to preface the ceremony :—" I beg your Majesty's pardon for mentioning in your august presence the name of so despicable a person, but this is the Jew (or Christian) So-and-so," as the case may be.

Slavery is an institution in Morocco, and slaves—like other commodities—are occasionally sold by auction in the public streets. It is not, however, the crying evil that it used to be in the Southern States of America, as, under Mahomedan rule, slaves have certain privileges not accorded by Christians, and are also, I believe, generally freed, after some years' servitude. They are, in fact, hardly in a worse position than their masters—everybody is a slave, except the Sultan. The Prime Minister may receive an intimation that he will be executed the next day, without any reason being assigned, except that "it is His Majesty's pleasure."

A visit to the interior of Morocco must be one of the most interesting expeditions that can be organized. I should be very glad if the means of undertaking it should ever fall in my way. For the present, I must bid the country adieu. The sea was rough on the day of my departure, and it was with difficulty that we managed to get from the small boat into the steamer. The passage occupied longer than usual, and the sea was frequently over the deck. The longest journeys have their endings, and we were at last in smooth water. Small boats landed us once more at Gibraltar.

CHAPTER VIII.

MALAGA.

Start in a Fog—Right of Property—Disadvantages of Malaga—Cathedral—Disturbances in 1872.

SOME of the finest coast scenery in Spain lies between Gibraltar and Malaga. It is seen to greatest advantage in the reverse direction. The rock soon becomes visible after leaving Malaga, and has the appearance of an island, the low-lying ground which connects it with the mainland being quite lost to view. Maravilla, about halfway between the two, is charmingly situated, and is remarkable for its mineral wealth.

The morning I left Gibraltar the fog was so thick that the small boat beat about the bay for half an hour before it could find the steamer; and after we had started a perpetual whistling had to be kept up to prevent collision with other vessels. Towards noon the fog partly cleared, and we were just able to discern the coast. Malaga, with its prominent-looking cathedral, was reached about eight hours from the time we left Gibraltar. Nowhere have I been so worried about luggage. I was not even allowed to disembark in the same boat with my portmanteau, a curtailment of my liberty, and the right to my property, of which I think the British authorities ought to be made aware.

Malaga is less interesting than any of the other Andalucian towns described. The immediate environs are ankle-deep in dust, and when there is a breeze, eyes, nose, ears and mouth, all get filled with this objectionable substance. The only building of any importance is the cathedral, the best external view of which is to be had from the bay; its size then appears to be larger than it really is, and its foundations to occupy half the area of the town. The style is

Corinthian, and the arrangements are after the usual Spanish pattern.

An instance of the habit of rapid burial practised on the Continent came before my notice whilst here. One evening, about an hour before sunset, I saw preparations being made for a funeral on rather a large scale. It appeared that the dead man had been in his usual health the evening before, and that he had died from the bursting of a blood-vessel during the early hours of the morning. Having heard that two persons had returned from the cemetery during the last cholera epidemic, after having been taken there as dead, it made one feel a little uncomfortable about the fate of the present individual. As the coffin passed, we all raised our hats out of respect for the dead; but who knows? we might only have been saluting the living!

Some three years since, I spent nearly a month in Malaga; and as it was my ill-luck to be present during an *émeute*, I will here give a short description of how Spaniards manage these things. King Amadeo, of recent memory, was at that time the recognised head of the Spanish people. The free and independent citizens of Malaga felt that the combination of a king and a foreigner was a little more than they could stand. A committee was formed, and their views made known to the public through the instrumentality of placards. "Down with the tyrant, and show yourselves to be men and Spaniards," was the patriotic appeal of these documents.

On the night of the 24th of November, 1872, a policeman happened to be tearing one of them down, when he was set upon by the mob, and so severely stabbed that he died the following day. On his way to the hospital, an attempt was made to attack the bearers; shots were fired, and one man wounded. From the 24th to the 28th the town was in the greatest state of excitement. Shopkeepers would, without any apparent warning that we could see, suddenly run up their shutters, and then, as nothing seemed to come of it, cautiously take them down again. A carabinero came to our hotel, to tell myself and friend that he had seen us out late at night. We admitted it.

"If you do not want to be shot," he added, "it would be more prudent to keep within."

On the afternoon of the 28th, we were walking by the sea, when we saw one of the most singular sights I ever witnessed. A crowd rushed pell mell down to the shore, and, jumping into the first boats they could seize, rowed out to sea, as if their lives depended upon it. The effect was so comic that we failed to perceive the gravity of the situation, but strolled on, to the end of the breakwater, and were quietly sitting down, watching the waves dashing over the rocks, when the sharp report of a musket roused us from our reverie. We jumped to our feet, and looked in the direction of the town. The report was soon followed by another, then another, and then a volley. Our first idea was to make for our hotel;

but upon second thoughts we decided that this course, though bold, was hardly discreet, as the fighting seemed to be in that neighbourhood. We walked some short distance along the breakwater, and joined a company of Spaniards, who looked upon the affair as nothing very extraordinary. One of them related how, during the last fight, a woman had been shot in the arm, standing in the very place where we now were.

At this juncture, I espied an officer belonging to the Spanish man-of-war, 'Alerta'; and appealed to him in our distress. His advice was to go on board his ship, which was then lying in the harbour; "for although we shall probably go into action, you will be safer there than on land." We thanked him, and were forthwith conveyed on board, and introduced to the captain. After expressing our gratitude at having found a shelter in his vessel, we awaited the arrival of the first engineer, a Scotchman. Under circumstances like these, the idea of meeting with a compatriot was more than usually agreeable. He turned out to be a man of the right sort; took us into his cabin, and, during our two days' stay, made us as comfortable as circumstances would permit.

As we were sufficiently near the shore to be within reach of the enemy's bullets, decks were cleared for action, guns run out, and every man stood to his post. All were prepared to die, rather than yield, when— discretion suggested that we should steam out of range. Second thoughts are always best! So we quietly lay a mile and a half from the shore, awaiting orders from the Captain-general, who was directing the operations on land.

With the exception of a regiment of cavalry riding up to the fray, we saw little of what was going on, the fighting being confined to the Alameda and inner streets. All Thursday night, the reports continued, and it was evident that some points were being hotly contested. About 3 on Friday morning it almost ceased, but began again with renewed vigour at daybreak.

In the afternoon, an alarm was raised, that the enemy was aiming at the 'Alerta.' The orders the captain had received were, not to reply unless attacked by artillery; and this, the insurgents seemed not to possess.

Friday evening showed one of those clear bright atmospheres, when the natural vision seems to be extended far beyond its usual limits, and which is a sure precursor of rain. The mountains round Tetuan in Morocco—some seventy or eighty miles distant—shone out, gilded by the setting sun. Malaga looked its best. And how shall I describe the sea on such a night? And then man must needs mar this hallowed scene with the reports of his infernal machines, carrying death to some and wounds to others. The Royalists had now established a battery just outside the town, and were engaged in shelling the rebel positions, as Sol descended into a sea of colour. Some of the missiles were badly charged, as they burst high up in the air, doing comparatively little damage.

Friday night was only a repetition of the previous one. Early on Saturday morning, the enemy endeavoured to seize a Government building; but some field guns unexpectedly opening upon them, they were driven back with considerable loss. A boat was seen to leave the shore, and make for the 'Alerta.' We were all anxious to know the news—it was an order to steam up the river, and co-operate with one of the forts. This looked like work; "and very nasty work too," as our friend the engineer said. "Going into action with a foreign enemy is one thing, but to shell a town to which we consider ourselves attached, and in which we most of us have our wives and families, is quite another. We did it in '69; and I did not like stirring out of my house for months afterwards, for fear a knife should be run into me." I felt very sorry for the officers; for revenge is a strong feeling in these southern countries, and the knife a very usual weapon for a defeated and exasperated party to employ. However, where stern duty calls, brave men must follow; so the anchor was being reluctantly weighed when another boat was descried. The order had been rescinded, and the 'Alerta' was to hasten with troops to Maravilla. This was a great relief to the ship's company, though it placed us two in rather an awkward plight. Our luggage was in Malaga, and we wished to rejoin it. The firing had become slack that morning, and the very idea of taking troops away argued a victory for the Royalists; so we begged the captain to let us land by the next boat; and, an opportunity soon occurring, after half an hour's row we were again in Malaga.

The streets were as still as in the dead of night; soldiers at every corner; not a civilian to be seen; the guards relieving one another at intervals being the only sounds. At our hotel we were met by the landlord and his wife, looking as happy as possible. They had had no idea of what had become of us. As for the insurgents, they had been driven out of every part of the town. They were now entrenched outside, and it was likely they would come to terms. Our rooms had been occupied by the soldiers, Thursday night, and the whole of Friday. Many of the windows were broken, and a church opposite bore several traces of recent bullets. The same day, the rebels were dispersed, and most of them fled into the country. Our property had been carefully stowed away, and the only loss I sustained was a box of cigarettes, which I conclude the soldiers took, to solace themselves with.

So ended this little affair. I never could obtain an exact estimate of the killed and wounded; but I believe it was not great, considering the amount of powder expended. One innocent victim I know to have been among the killed—a poor deaf old woman was shot by a sentry for not answering the challenge, which she probably did not hear. The following story is often related as a reason why Spain should never be otherwise than in a disturbed state:—A Spanish king, when dying, was visited by the Mother of God.

"What will you for your country?" she asked.

"Handsome men and fair women," replied the monarch.

"It is granted."

"A beautiful climate—the fruits of the earth abundant," etc., etc.

"All granted."

"A good Government."

"No," said the sainted visitor; "for then the very angels would leave Heaven to come and dwell in Spain."

CHAPTER IX.

GRANADA.

Coaching in Spain—Alhambra—Sacramonte and its Martyrs —The Canary Bird—Safety of the Streets—Almeria— Cartagena—Arrested—Spanish Politeness.

As I shall not go to Granada this time, I will subjoin an account of a visit I paid to it, a few days after the incidents related above. The distance from Malaga is, I believe, about one hundred and twenty English miles; and yet the time taken by the combined railway and *diligence* used to be nearly twelve hours, the through train leaving Malaga in the afternoon. For the first few miles, the line passes through orchards of orange-trees,—at this season of the year covered with fruit; and then pierces a rocky mountain range, where the scenery becomes bold and striking. At

Bobadilla, a branch railway conducts to Las Salinas, and at this latter euphonious-sounding place we got into a rickety omnibus drawn by six animals. In the darkness, it was difficult to say whether they were horses or mules. Each was provided with a name, which the driver would shout out at the top of his voice, whenever he wished to bring that particular animal to a sense of his duty.

We dashed along, quite regardless of consequences, swaying backwards and forwards like a pendulum—at one time splashing through a young river, the rate at which we were going, I am convinced, alone preventing our over-turning. Suddenly we stop. Carlists! Brigands! Alphonsists! Republicans! What can this be? We are prepared for the worst—only let it come quickly—anything is better than suspense. "Happy thought!"—stopped to change animals! I now put my head out of the window with an alacrity which, a minute ago, I should have thought highly venturesome. It was about midnight, and an oil lamp was burning in front of a little inn. Whether my conjecture was right or not, I do not know. We went on again, and at 1 a.m. reached Loja, a large town in communication with Granada by rail—one train daily—or, I should more correctly say, nightly. This leaves on the arrival of the *diligence*, and the return train starts at 2 a.m. I think it would somewhat astonish the British public if the only trains between Bristol and Bath were to start respectively at 1 a.m. and 2 a.m.! Happily for us, our lines are not in the hands of Spanish officials. The cold on the night I am alluding to was piercing, as is always the case in winter at Granada, owing to its great elevation.

Of all the large towns in Spain, this is in nearly every respect the most interesting. Besides its magnificent natural position, in full view of the Sierra Nevada, it was the last seat and the last stronghold of the Moorish dynasty. No one need ever regret the time and labour spent in reaching

Granada. The first day I naturally gave up to the Alhambra—the finest of Spain's palaces, and the richest of her treasures. An avenue of elms leads up to this matchless gem of art. The Patio de Los Leones is the first court; and in it, the spectator begins to realize the great taste and wonderful artistic genius developed by the Moors in the zenith of their civilization. Room succeeds to room. It would be difficult at this distance of time to describe each in detail; but the general effect produced on the mind is one I shall never forget. Generaliffe, the winter palace, is far inferior.

The Cartuja, a suppressed monastery, is rich in marbles; and its chapel is considered very fine. Another suppressed monastery is Sacramonte, now an ecclesiastical seminary for the training of young men for holy orders. I went with a Spanish friend, who carried a letter of introduction to one of the priests. The reverend gentleman shook hands cordially; and then, producing some cigarettes, suggested that all should light up. When we had finished smoking, business began. He conducted us through all the different parts of the establishment, explaining the purpose of each. We descended below the surface of the earth, and came to a small chapel. " Here," said our cicerone, " seven martyrs once suffered." We stood for a few moments gazing, wrapt in profound meditation. The priest knelt forward; and, gathering a little dust which there lay, presented a small quantity to each. It would have been more acceptable to anyone wishing to lay the foundations of a private *relicario*, than to myself who, not being accustomed to handle things so precious, was a little puzzled to know what to do with it. We were subsequently introduced to the rector of the college, looked at some pictures, and then departed, seeing on our return "the mountain of the sun," and "the river of gold." Could places bearing such high-flown names be otherwise than beautiful?

On Saturday, the 7th of December,

a rising was expected in the town; and the troops were under arms all night. Sunday, the 8th, being the festival of the Conception of our Blessed Lady—patroness of Spain—all well-disposed persons went to church. At the cathedral, high mass was celebrated, with all those accompaniments befitting so great an occasion; the archbishop being the celebrant. He is a little man, and, when pontifically vested, looks nearly as broad as he is long. At the "*Domine non sum dignus*" a canary began to sing—or my ears deceived me. Again the archbishop, striking his breast, expressed his unworthiness to receive the sacrament (a statement which was, no doubt, perfectly correct); and again the bird sang.

> "But hark! above the organ's notes is heard
> The soft sweet singing of a gentle bird—
> One of that brood which haunts Canary's isles,
> Where nature shines in all her beauteous smiles:
> Sweet birthplace of the precious bird who wings
> His course along her shore—and who now sings,
> As if he too would like to blend his hymn
> With the angelic choir of Seraphim.

Sing on, sweet bird ! sing on thy gentle lay!
May angels, hastening on their homeward way,
Cleaving through earth, and air, and sea, and sky,
Straight to the mighty throne of God most high,
Remembering thee—may they before Him say
How thou did'st warble forth thy little lay,
And tried'st in thine own sweet way, to sing
Thy heartfelt praises to th' Eternal King.

And there,—before that bright and awful throne,
Before which heaven and earth shall one day come—
Thy song of purity a place may find
Denied to many, though of human kind,
And thy reward, a cherub's form may be,
In those bless'd regions of eternity,
Where nought is heard but sound of praise and prayer,
Mingled like incense floating on the air."

An American once went to the cathedral to hear the midnight mass on Christmas Eve. Returning to his hotel he lost his way, and on inquiring from a passer-by, was conducted to the avenue of elms leading to the Alhambra, and there robbed of all he possessed save his shirt. When at last he reached home, the maid-servant was so affrighted at his white appearance, that she ran away, shrieking, "Una fantasma! una fantasma!" I give this anecdote to show how safe Granada is after dark.

The cold before and after sunset is intense, and makes the two o'clock morning start still more uninviting. However, as there was no other train, I made the best of it, and arrived at Malaga at the same hour in the afternoon, having had to walk for about half a mile over a portion of railway, which either the weather or one of the numerous *partidas* had destroyed.

The steamer for Almeria generally leaves in the evening, and so one loses the only chance of seeing the Sierra Nevada chain from the sea; a view said to be very beautiful. At Almeria we remained a day. I am quite tired of describing Spanish scenery: it is the same story over and over again; and the surroundings of Almeria—unlike those of Granada—form no exception to the general barrenness which, added to the whiteness of the houses, makes it very trying to the eyes. In the town, which is built in a semi-Moorish style, there are one or two palms, and the usual number of *cafés*. The beach, which in civilized places is such a delightful resort, is in Spain the receptacle for all the refuse of the neighbourhood; and as the Mediterranean has but little tide, the odours exhaled render the sea, within a mile or two of a town, anything but agreeable.

The steamer left the same evening, and the morning of the 13th of October, 1875, saw me in Cartagena. Although the vessel had come from a Spanish port, all passengers' luggage was examined, just as if we had come from France or Italy. These little annoyances—nothing in themselves—render travelling in Spain very disagreeable. Cartagena lies in a kind of horse-shoe bay, the hilly country around being precisely similar to that in the neighbourhood of Almeria. It had recently been the scene of considerable fighting between two classes of Republicans—the adherents of the then Government, and the *Intransigientes*,—the traces of which were still visible in many parts. The house opposite the one in which I was staying was roofless and windowless, and in a room on the first floor a cannon-ball was peacefully lying. I entered a church under repair, and, in a small chapel on the right, saw—I do not wish to be irreverent—what looked exactly like a portion of Madame Tussaud's waxwork show. There were fifteen life-size figures of saints. I suppose in the ordinary course of things these fifteen figures would have been spread over the church, and their ludicrous conglomerate effect thereby avoided. A man and woman were kneeling before the altar. A little boy advanced and spread white cloths over the head of the one and the shoulders of the other. I thought to myself, "This looks suspicious;" but when I saw the priest join their hands, etc., etc., I thought to myself, "Poor fellow! it is all up with him now! He's done for."

I omitted to mention that at seven o'clock the first morning after my arrival, whilst I was still in bed, a gendarme, a civilian, and the chambermaid entered my room. The first of these put a running string of questions as to whence I came, whither I was going, what my business might be, with many others of an equally impertinent nature. When he had made himself fully acquainted with my whole history, past, present, and future, he departed, accompanied by the civilian and the chambermaid.

The same day, walking just outside the walls with an Englishman, we were both arrested, and marched through the town to the official residence of Señor Don Juez, Judge of the First Instance; a soldier keeping an eye upon us all the time, to see that we did not escape *en route*. At the court we were kept some twenty minutes, and should probably have been detained much longer, but for my friend telling some of the officials that he had to catch a steamer, and should hold them responsible for the consequences should he fail to do so. We were then admitted into the august presence of Señor Don Juez; simply to be told, in the most polished language—without any attempt at apology—that we might go.

Spanish politeness and courtesy are proverbial; and, if words can be always taken for what they mean—justly so. The common form of address is in the third person, with " Usted " or " Ustedes," which means something like " your grace," or " your graces." " Will your Grace go for a walk this morning ? "—the compliment which such language would otherwise convey being rather diminished when one hears the same applied indiscriminately to waiters, cab-drivers, and boatmen. " I kiss the hand of your Grace," is a favourite expression on parting, or to wind up a letter; but notwithstanding the number of times I have heard it said, I never yet saw it done. "At the feet of your Grace " is a very proper thing for a gentleman to say to a lady on taking his departure. "I kiss the hand, señor," is the reply. In speaking of another man, it is usual to say "this knight" ("este caballero") instead of "this gentleman." When a visitor enters a Spanish house, the host will place everything at his disposition; whilst he, of course, being equally polite, never avails himself of this liberality. The farce is still farther carried on, when a man writes to his friend, and dates his letter "from the house of your Grace," starting on the assumption that all his possessions have already been made over to his correspondent. A polite Spaniard will also always offer to give anything which his friend may happen to admire; but the latter is never expected to accept the same.

Cartagena was the last town in Spain at which I stayed; and I do not very much care if it remain so.

CHAPTER X.

VALENCIA AND BARCELONA.

Alicante—The Bull-fight at Valencia—Barcelona—Cette—Nîmes—Varieties.

Before leaving for Algeria, I will say a few words upon the remaining towns on the eastern coast, and describe that thoroughly Spanish institution—a bull-fight; in order to do which, I shall have to encroach upon my 1872 reminiscences. The steamer leaving the Bay of Cartagena, starts as usual in the evening; steers north-east; and, early next morning drops anchor at Alicante, a small town, the port of Madrid, also situated in a hilly country. I have recently heard that it contains a good hotel, and that invalids sometimes spend the winter there. Some miles distant is Elche, where are the finest palm plantations in Europe.

The steamer again starts in the evening;

and arrives the next morning at Grao, the port of Valencia, which is distant some four miles, and accessible by train. Valencia is an important commercial town, and contains a remarkably fine cathedral; and a bull-ring—one of the largest in Spain. Exhibitions generally take place on Sunday afternoons in summer and autumn. In the morning, a tame cow is paraded through the streets, with military honours, to attract popular attention to the fact that a fight is about to take place. One occurring whilst we were there, my friend and myself turned into the great building prepared for the occasion, a little before 3. It resembled in shape the Colosseum at Rome, and as far as my recollections go, seemed to be as large.

The grand procession of bandilleros, picuederos, and matadores—all in their medieval dresses, was picturesque; but this was the only part of the performance that could be designated by any other word than disgusting. After one or two non-fighting bulls had come in and kept the company amused until all were assembled, the real business of the afternoon began. The president gave the signal, and the bull to be slaughtered entered the arena. At first he looked a little scared, and ran about without any particular object. The bandilleros came in with coloured cloths, and flourished them in the eyes of the animal. It is well known that nothing incenses a bull so much as bright colours; so, instead of paying any attention to the men, all his energies were occupied with tearing and rending the offending calico. When ten minutes or so had been spent in this tolerably harmless amusement, small iron goads, to which pieces of coloured ribbon had been attached for the sake of ornament, were thrown at him, and sticking in his flesh, caused him so much pain that his efforts to rend what he no doubt considered the cause of it all—the coloured rags—were redoubled.

Another ten minutes, and then came the

picuederos—men on horseback, carrying long lances with which to pierce the bull. They are capitally protected, their legs being cased in leather about an inch thick, having, it is said, a thin metal lining, quite impervious to the strongest horn; whilst their bodies are too high to be in much danger. The horses—wretched animals no longer fit for work, bought for a mere song, and fed up for the last few days that they might not present quite such a meagre appearance—come into the arena without the slightest protection, and blinded on the side nearest the bull. What follows is not difficult to foresee. In the present instance, the bull charged, the picuedero missed his aim, and a large hole in the breast of the horse was the sole result. Perpetual spurring brought the poor animal again to the front; another charge, and this time its entrails protruded through the gaping wound. Bleeding profusely, it walked on a few paces and then fell. The picuedero dismounted, and as neither beating nor spurring could induce it to rise, it was left to die; and the bull's attention attracted to another horse, when a similar scene was again enacted.

What surprised me most was the delight which the women, as well as the men, took in these sickening scenes. To see that noblest of all animals, the horse, lacerated by the bull's horns, and quivering under spur and lash, caused such a shout of joy as made the very building ring with its echo. When a man was in the slightest danger the greatest efforts were made with all the coloured paraphernalia to distract the bull, and give him time to reach the parapet some four feet high, with a ledge for the foot half-way up, which divides the arena from the spectators. But when the bull, catching sight of one of the wounded horses lying on the ground, made for it, not a hand was raised; and an exulting cry of delight from the excited audience was the approval he received when, by the sheer force of his horns, he raised the dying animal to its feet. The horse staggered for two or three paces and then fell. A few minutes afterwards I saw the body quiver for a second, and then I believe its pains were over.

The closing scene is the entrance of the matadores—experts in the art of bull-fighting. They are the favourites of the people, and, like celebrated actors and actresses, the heads of the profession take a high position; it is even said that the late queen was enamoured of one of them. They enter the arena on foot, armed with a small sword and a coloured cloth. It is their business to go up to the bull, now weak with loss of blood and exhausted with fighting, and give him the *coup de grace*. During the earlier part of the proceedings, the matador (a euphonism for a butcher) watches to see if he has any peculiarities—whether in tossing he inclines his head to the right or the left, and to which colour he has the strongest aversion; and with the knowledge thus obtained, he can approach with tolerable safety. On this occasion, the matador stuck his sword into the bull's forehead, but not piercing a vital part, the animal ran away with the blade sticking in him. There was, however, not much difficulty in recovering it, he being by this time so weak that he contented himself with acting strictly on the defensive. In a few minutes more he fell and died. Mules gaudily harnessed now came in, and being attached to the dead or dying animals, galloped round the arena and so flourished them out. Thus ended the first act, which lasted about an hour.

The Spanish thirst for blood was, however, not yet satisfied. Another bull was driven in, and the same disgusting performance re-enacted, with the exception that this one not being thought to show the courage of his predecessor, fireworks were thrown at him, which, sticking in his flesh continued burning for several minutes.

When the second bull was dead, a cow was let loose into the ring, and was the amusement of a crowd of men and boys who had gathered there, in order to show their agility in escaping from its horns. One man, not quite so expert as his fellows, was knocked down and injured. The crowd gathered round him, to pick him up; but the cow, seeing this unusual number of persons congregated in one place, boldly charged them. A *sauve qui peut* followed, and the injured man was left to shift for himself. A boy endeavouring to get over the parapet, received some assistance from the cow, who bundled him over rather more quickly than he would otherwise have gone.

Nothing, that I can see, can be urged in defence of bull-fights. They are a disgrace to the nineteenth century, and a stigma upon civilization. The continued repetition of these sights keeps up in the people the old thirst for blood, which might otherwise, in course of time, die out. And if the Spanish Government is too weak, or too careless, to suppress these exhibitions in the interests of humanity, might it not be as well were a foreign power to impress upon Spain her duty in this respect? England can interfere with the internal administration of Zanzibar, and tell the ruler of that country that he is no longer to keep slaves: could she not look a little nearer home, and tell the ministers of Alfonso XII. that they are no longer to allow bull-fights?

Valencia is much visited in winter by the Madrileños, who come here to seek a milder climate. It has pretty gardens;—not much else, except the cathedral already alluded to. It is a long journey from here to Barcelona, whether taken by sea or land; and as the Carlists are frequently cutting the line, the former is preferable. A solitary palm or two, in the neighbourhood of Valencia, is, perhaps, the last the traveller will see on his journey north.

Barcelona, the capital of Catalonia, and numerically the second city in the kingdom, is styled by some, a "*petit Paris.*" It has not, however, much in common with its great prototype, except some fine streets and a *Rambla*, corresponding to a boulevard. The cathedral is not considered so good as many of the others; it has, nevertheless, some interesting tombs. The Opera House is one of the largest in Europe; and there I heard some second-class singing in Italian.

The steamer bound for Cette skirts the land, affording fine views of the mountainous coast scenery, and the little villages scattered here and there along the shore. The Pyrenees next become visible, and in twenty hours Cette is reached. The railway from here to Nîmes—two hours—passes through a flat country. The first station, Montpellier, is an ancient watering-place; now superseded by Nice, Pau, and Mentone. Then come several unimportant stations; and, finally, Nîmes, described hereafter.

Travelling in Spain is always slow. The trains are punctual; the steamers quite the reverse. On one occasion I purchased a ticket for a steamer advertised to start at noon, on which was written that passengers must embark at least an hour beforehand. Being one of my first experiences, I religiously went on board at eleven o'clock; and when, at a quarter past three, the vessel steamed out of the port, the golden flag of Spain flying from her stern was a quite sufficient explanation. Charges by the steamers are very high for short distances, but the fare from Seville to Marseilles or Santander is comparatively small.

The ideas which sometimes get about, that there is nothing to eat in Spain that does not swim in oil, or smell of garlic—are about as true as that Englishmen always eat their meat raw. No one who keeps to the large towns—unless a very great gourmand indeed—need have the slightest fear on the score of food.

The postal arrangements are anything but satisfactory. A very small per centage of letters ever arrive at their destination—at least that is my experience. As a test of expedition, I posted a letter at Malaga, at the principal office, addressed "Poste Restante, Malaga." The next day, inquiring for my letter, a few yards from the place where I put it in, I was told it had not arrived; and it was only on the fifth day that it was given me. If letters take five days in travelling from one part of the Post-office to another, what must they take in going across the country?

Most of the towns are provided with theatres—mean establishments. The scenes are seldom changed; and actors and actresses do nothing but make long-winded speeches at each other. I did not often honour their performances with my presence, as I object to doing penance when on a holiday tour.

Spring and autumn are the best times for the Peninsula; indeed, the other seasons should be carefully avoided. For cathedrals, visit Cordova, Burgos, and Seville; for Moorish palaces—Granada and Seville; for pictures—Madrid; for natural scenery—Granada; and for a winter climate—Malaga.

CHAPTER XI.

ORAN.

Two notable Men—Oran—French and Arabs—The Mosque —Koubbas—Mostaganem—École Française—The native Court—The Arab Quarter.

WHILE at Cartagena, I had the good fortune to make the acquaintance of two rather notable men; the one, an Algerian Deputy to the National Assembly; the other, the acting Administrator of the town and district of Mostaganem. The former gave me some valuable advice as to the country I was about to visit, and then went his way to join in those stormy scenes for which the French Assembly has ever been noted. The latter invited me to his home, and promised to show me Mostaganem and its environs; which, from his official position, he was better able to do than anyone else. Such an offer was too good to be refused, although that town was a little out of the route I had at first intended to take. A French lady and her daughter, just on the eve of visiting Algeria, were invited to join the party.

So, on the evening of the 16th of October, we four embarked on the French vessel 'Ajaccio,' bound for Oran. The first thing which greeted our arrival on board, was dancing on the quarter-deck—a fact which in itself would have gone far to establish the nationality of the vessel, had any proof been wanting. The night was passed at sea; and the morning found us at Oran, a city of no small importance, the capital of a province, and containing a population of some 40,000. It presents the singular appearance common to all such towns, which strikes the traveller at every turn—namely, the mixture of European and Oriental. The Frenchman—dressed in the latest Parisian style, gesticulating with that vivacity for which his nation is so remarkable—walks side by side with the placid, imperturbable Arab, in his long, flowing, Eastern garb of pure white, looking more like the silent inhabitant of the land of spirits than the living flesh and blood of the nineteenth century; the black descendant of Ham, who, after so many generations of slavery, at last freed from his bondage, now lives on terms of goodwill and fellowship with another race, perhaps equally oppressed and equally enduring—the Jew; the soldiers and the gendarmerie of France, with the Turco and the Spahis; the church side by side with the mosque, as if the cross and crescent, after so long a warfare, were at last going hand in hand, following the same path, and alike elevating men's hearts to God.

We took a carriage and drove round the town, visiting the beautiful promenade, and the celebrated mosque. On arriving at its entrance, two French officers—with a taste hardly to be commended—had gone in without taking off their shoes. This led to an altercation between them and the Arabs within; and to their being eventually expelled. As there is no idea of an altar or a sacrifice in the Mahomedan religion, the interior of their places of worship is plain and unadorned when compared with a Christian church. There is little, in fact, to be seen, except the faithful at their devotions, prostrating themselves in the direction of Mecca. The faces of some are quite a study; there is written there so unmistakably the fatalism of their creed, "God is great—His sacred will be done." And so they let time and mundane affairs go their way.

In the course of the day, we visited some sulphur springs in the environs, but found them closed. I do not suppose we lost much.

Leaving Oran the next morning, at 6 a.m., we took the train to Relizane. A few camels visible in the distance reminded us that we had quitted Europe; otherwise, there was nothing special to note on the route. The line passes through a flat uninteresting country, hardly less barren than Spain. At Relizane, we breakfasted; and then proceeded by *diligence* to Mostaganem. These vehicles are generally well appointed, well-horsed, and go at a tolerable pace. On our way we passed several Koubbas—small white buildings, generally the tomb of an Arab saint, which, when large enough to admit of entrance, form a sort of oratory or house of prayer for the wanderer and the pilgrim, serving him in the place of the mosque. The aloes and the Barbary fig seem here to flourish in all their native luxuriance; and, as in the south of Spain, form the hedges between different properties. At length, after six hours of misery—for travelling in a *diligence* is always such, in my opinion—we reached Mostaganem; and were not long in installing ourselves, (as the French say,) dining, and going to bed.

The next day we were visited by the Administrator, and one of his Arab servants; and at once started to see the lions of the place. The first thing visited was the École Française. Little French and Arab children sat side by side, learning the same lessons from the same master. People in England, who hear so much about school-boards and religious difficulties, and who are taught to believe it all but impossible for Churchman and Dissenter to sit side by side, would be truly astonished to see Christian and Mahomedan associating in such perfect harmony.

Children from three years old and upwards were pointing out letters on a black board; those of about seven seemed to have acquired a proficiency in what have been popularly called "the three R's,"—reading, 'riting, and 'rithmetic. A very intelligent Arab boy of about ten, stepped forward, and read from a French book, with an accuracy and fluency that it would be difficult to match in an English school. Then a French boy related a story in Arabic; for which, I am ashamed to say, we were not much the wiser, until he translated it into French. The school is voluntary, and the education secular. French and Arab parents do or do not send their children, as they think fit.

We next went to the mosque, which is similar to other buildings of the same class, and were told by our guide that Christians are not allowed to ascend the minaret.

The native court is presided over by an Arab judge called the Cadi. It is his province to try, in the first instance, all disputes respecting property: criminal cases are not brought under his notice. On our entry, all business was suspended, and the court rose, out of respect. The Administrator begged the judge to continue. After shaking hands, and requesting us to be seated, he consented to do so. The question was as to the boundary of a certain field, and was being generally discussed by the judge, the clerks, and the parties concerned; each having something to say in turn. Here again our want of knowledge of Arabic prevented our appreciating what might otherwise have been an interesting conversation. Should either of the parties feel dissatisfied with the judgment here given, there is an appeal to the court of First Instance; and from this latter, to a court held in the principal town of each province; and finally, the case may go before the Court of Cassation at Paris. From what I could learn, the Cadis are in the habit of receiving bribes, and delivering judgment in favour of the largest donor. For this reason, they are mistrusted by the Arabs who, for the most part, prefer to go before the French authorities, rather than before their own judges.

Having again shaken hands with the Cadi and several of the officials of the court, we went in search of the Arab quarter, which is quite distinct from the European, and presents the usual appearance of a small native town—dirty, narrow streets, a total absence of vehicles, and cross-legged Arabs seated in their small shops. Here I was presented with a flower. In European countries it is usual to make such offerings to the ladies of the party; but in Barbary, women are not thought much of, honour and precedence being always given to the male sex.

In the afternoon we took a carriage, and drove to the ancient residence of an Arab chief. The place, if kept in repair, might have been worth seeing, but in its present condition it certainly was not. The yelping of half-a-dozen curs heralded our approach, and these unmusical sounds were kept up until we were fairly out of sight.

The next day we were to be the guests of Mohamed Ben Mocktit Ben Ahmed. The night after this, we were to pass far away, amongst those distant hills, now scarcely visible; with nothing but a tent to shield us from the inclemencies of the weather, and dogs and guns from the ravages of wild beasts.

CHAPTER XII.

A NIGHT WITH ARABS.

Ein Tedlitz—Mr. Mocktit—The Mysterious Dahra—Arab Saddles—Crossing a River—Compliments—Dinner—The Tadjin—A Night Walk—The Tents—"To Bed but not to Sleep"—Sunrise—Return to Ein Tedlitz—Equine Ailments—The Tortoise.

WE rose early the next morning, and spent the time in seeing the European portion of Mostaganem. It is built much in the same style as the other Algerian towns: a large handsome square, in the middle of which generally stands the modern church—the square and the principal streets leading from it being arcaded after the manner of an Italian city, forming a delightful promenade in wet weather.

About noon we started on our expedition, and being four in number, comfortably filled the interior of a carriage, which was to take us to Ein Tedlitz, a drive of about three hours. Vegetation was scanty, excepting for the cactus tribe; and the road, for a great part of the way, passed through a sandy country, in which tortoises abound. At the village we were met by our host, Mohamed Ben Mocktit Ben Ahmed, who had brought with him a number of horses, mules, and servants.

As the road here ended, our carriage was useless, so, mounting the horses, we rode in the direction of the Dahra mountains—" the mysterious Dahra," as they were so long called, and might still have been, had not recent exploration dispelled this, as it does most other mysteries.

We rode for upwards of an hour through hilly country, our host taking the lead, and the rear being brought up by an escort of mounted Arabs. The pace never exceeded a slight trot, as several of the servants were on foot; besides which, the ladies had no saddles, being seated sideways on horsecloths, and under such circumstances a gallop would no doubt have produced a spill. I was in a Turkish saddle, but having been somewhat accustomed to this kind of thing in Morocco, was not much inconvenienced.

We reached the banks of the river Chelif, which had to be crossed. There was no bridge. Mohamed Ben Mocktit Ben Ahmed (whom I shall call for short, "Mr. Mocktit") had ordered his boat to await our arrival. We dismounted and got in; and some natives, dressed in the most scanty of costumes, proceeded to pull us across. The river was muddy and shallow; it could not have exceeded three feet in its deepest part. When we were safely deposited on the other side, the boat returned for the saddles and horsecloths. After some difficulty, the horses and mules were induced, one by one, to take the water, and having reached the opposite bank in safety, were re-saddled. The path now became wilder and more hilly. About sunset, we saw in a valley below the tents in which we were to pass the night. On arriving there, our host bade us regard the country in every direction, as far as we could see. "It *was* his; *now* it was ours. Would that he had the whole of Africa, that he might give it us! Would that he had tens of thousands of horses, that they might all die in our service! Would that he had hundreds of wives, that we might take them all! *Then* would he be happy!"

Compliments with Orientals must be strong to go down. It was now our turn, although it would have been difficult indeed to out-do what had already been said. We could only reply that nothing had been left undone to insure our happiness and comfort; and that, wherever we went, in France, England, Italy, we would tell of the cordial welcome with which we had been received. In conclusion, "Were we not the guests of Mohamed Ben Mocktit Ben Ahmed, and was not that in itself a pleasure for the rest of our lives?" On hearing that, the good man exclaimed that "his soul mounted to the heavens!"

We entered the tent, luxuriously spread with carpets and richly embroidered cushions, and having placed ourselves in a sort of semi-circle at the farther end—the two ladies in the middle, the Administrator and myself at either side, each reclining on two pillows—awaited the repast. Coffee was first served, in small cups, each placed inside a larger one; the reason of this being that the first, containing the coffee, was too hot to hold; whilst the outer one, not being in immediate contact with the heated fluid, was comparatively cool. An entire sheep, roasted, was now brought in, at the end of a pole, in order that it might be inspected. When we had satisfied ourselves as to the nature of the animal, two servants stepped forward, and in our presence twisted off the head; and another, taking a hatchet, separated the ribs; after which, it was placed before us, and we were bidden to begin.

Our host, knowing our habits, had provided us with forks; but we, being determined "when in Turkey, to do as the Turkeys do," declined these novel inventions, and resolved for once to live in a state of simplicity. So each, tearing off the piece which most accorded with his or her fancy, began to eat. I do not exaggerate when I say that it was delicious. The Administrator warned us not to partake too freely, as other dishes were coming, and if we did not patronise all, Mr. Mocktit would be offended. The whole sheep is called, in Arabic, *Messhouar*. It always begins all grand entertainments. For less distinguished visitors the fore-quarter only is served; it is then called *Gachouch*.

If we had not known that Arab etiquette does not allow the host to eat at the same time as his guest, we should have been surprised to see Mr. Mocktit waiting upon us, instead of joining us in our onset on the mutton. When we had finished with the sheep, it was placed before some Arabs of distinction, at the farther end of the tent.

From them it went to the grade below, and so on, until it reached the servants, and finally the dogs. Each dish, as we finished with it, descended the social scale, in the same order. The *cherbaa*—or soup—came next, and was anything but unpalatable. Mr. Mocktit, knowing the European proclivity for wine, had procured some bottles of excellent Hermitage, which were opened and passed round. Then came the *Touadjin*—in the singular, *Tadjin*. The *Tadjin* is a sort of mixture of vegetables, meat, fowl, or eggs. The composition of each varies; thus, the first may contain beans, rice, and fowl; the second, veal, cauliflower, and potatoes; and so on. It is served with what resembles in size and form an ordinary pocket-handkerchief, made of some kind of meal. This is first used to catch hold of the different portions of the *Tadjin*, and is then eaten itself, with the piece it has taken up, instead of bread. The number of these dishes may vary from one upwards, according to the nature of the repast, and the rank of the guest. On the present occasion, there were eight. After the first two or three, our appetites were quite satisfied, and it was with difficulty that we could do our duty to the remaining five or six—for my part, they were partaken of simply *pro causâ formæ*; although, no doubt, as they descended into other hands they found eager recipients.

Now came the dessert, which consisted of several kinds of fruit (grapes of course being included), biscuits steeped in honey, and biscuits *au naturel*. A delay of half-an-hour usually occurs between the dessert and the *cous-couss*, which always concludes a dinner. It is the ordinary Arab dish, and is made of a certain cereal resembling rice (for which I at first mistook it), and answers to bread in England, or macaroni in Italy. A bowl of soup, or—in the Province of Oran—honey, is occasionally turned over it, before being served. It would not have been refused by a hungry man, although, at this stage of the proceedings, we ate it simply out of curiosity.

Coffee was handed round—first to the ladies, the Administrator having hinted to Mr. Mocktit, before the beginning of dinner, that with us it is customary to serve them first: he looked a little astonished, but did as suggested. Water was then poured over our hands—by no means a superfluous ceremony, considering the uses to which they had been put.

We took a stroll with our host. As the moon was not yet risen, it was quite dark, and a lantern-bearer went before. By this means we were enabled to investigate what was to form our shelter for the night. The tent of honour was small, and of circular construction; it was temporarily put up, and on our departure would be struck. Those inhabited by Mr. Mocktit and his retinue were rather huts than tents, being permanent, made of earth and bent boughs of trees: to enter them, stooping to a considerable extent was absolutely necessary. One contained Mr. Mocktit's two wives. The ladies of the party were admitted to see these dames; and from their account, Mrs. Mocktit No. 2. was very beautiful, although inclining to be stout; while Mrs. Mocktit No. 1., who had passed her teens, had already become too stout to be prepossessing.

A truly patriarchal way this of living! Thus Abraham lived of old, thousands of years ago, with his sheep and his cattle, his men-servants and his maid-servants. Our host, with his long white flowing dress, and his kindly face beaming good-will on all around, might well have been taken for the venerable Patriarch himself—the father of Isaac. And here—miles from any European habitation—surrounded by the very people whose country Europeans had taken—we laid down to rest; and for my part, I felt as secure as in my bed in town. We were now their guests—having eaten under the roof of their chief—and as such, to harm us would be sacrilege. The tent was given up to the ladies, the Administrator and myself turning into one of the huts; at the farther corner of which, a carpet was laid upon Mother Earth—a pillow and a blanket comprised the rest of our bedding. How primitive it all was! By the flickering of the lantern I espied at the other end a sheep, and one or two Arabs at their devotions,—standing, kneeling, prostrating themselves, standing again—adoring after their fashion the Unseen Ruler of all things, the God of Heaven.

Up to this time, all had been "*couleur de rose*—the strange contrast to usual habits—the reception—the repast—the walk in the still African night, broken only by the piercing cry of the jackal, the barking of dogs, and occasionally the bleating of a sheep. And now we sought the rest for which we were so well prepared; but alas! a terrible thorn grew straight out of this rose of primitiveness. No sooner had we lain down, than fleas began their deadly work. I soon perceived that not a moment's sleep were we to have that night. They literally swarmed; and to have executed a dozen or so, even had it been possible, would only have been like a drop drained from the ocean. So nothing was to be done but to assume for that evening the Arab fatalism, which lets the will of Allah take its course, without effort to avert it. Occasionally, I admit, I became restive, and tried to inflict terrible vengeance upon my tormentors; but all in vain. I got up, and went out. A few Arabs chatting round a fire, and the dogs regaling themselves on the remains of our dinner, was all I saw for my pains. I returned to lie down, and found myself beside a dog who, for greater privacy, had entered the hut, to finish his bone in peace. I spoke to my companion. We sympathized, but were powerless to aid each other. He related previous experiences—I was happy to say this was my first; and in saying so, truly longed for the breaking of the day. At last—yes, at last —it came. The Arabs were hastening to eat; for this being the sacred month of Ramadan, no food could be taken between sunrise and sunset. I got up, and climbed the side of a hill, in order to see the sunrise. Night was fast disappearing. Not only the east, but the west also, glowed with crimson. The mountain tops first catch the light of the coming sun—slowly and silently his rays steal down each slope, until all alike are bathed in one radiant sea of glory.

How refreshing is coffee in the early morning! especially if one has not passed a particularly good night. The Arabs know how to prepare it. Their method is somewhat different from ours, but the result is much better.

To horse! was the order of the day, as we had a long ride before us. Mr. Mocktit was going to conduct us back by a new and very much longer route, in order that we might see something of the country. So each mounted betimes his Arab steed. The Barbary horses are a long-enduring race; they do a great deal more work than would be got out of their English brethren, and are not so loved by their masters as generally represented—at least, the affection does not show itself in good treatment. The spurs which the Arabs use are unnecessarily large, and must cause great torture to the animals, whose sides are frequently bleeding. Some short time since, an Arab killed his horse with one dig from these huge spurs, which are more like the spikes for driving elephants than what we are usually accustomed to call by that name.

We passed many a hill and many a dale; then, riding along the muddy banks of the Chelif, came to a village. Crossing the river, we began to ascend on the other side, when one of the horses was taken ill. The poor animal lay down and rolled on the ground for a few minutes, and then seemed for a time to be all right, until the spasms came on again. The Arabs appeared to be acquainted with the disease; and when we arrived at the village of Ein Tedlitz, applied the following (as they pretend, infallible) remedy. A charge of gunpowder is fired into the nostrils of the affected animal; he is then put to a full gallop for a short distance; after this, they say he is quite well. This treatment seems cruel and barbarous in the extreme, but possibly the counter-irritation produced may tend to work a cure. I saw this particular horse after the application, but cannot say whether he was benefited.

At Ein Tedlitz, we lunched; and afterwards amused ourselves with a tortoise which had been picked up on the sands close by. I hate reptiles of every description; but one of the ladies took a great fancy to this one, and was anxious to take him home; which project was, however, abandoned, to my great relief, and the tortoise escaped the pleasure of a tour in Algeria, and a subsequent visit to Paris.

The same evening we returned to Mostaganem, and passed a more peaceful night than we had done in the huts.

CHAPTER XIII.

MOSTAGANEM TO ALGIERS.

Bousian—Visit to the Prison—A Jovial Criminal—Fever—
Newly Created Villages—Blidah—Visit to the Monkeys—
Stalactite Cave—Medeah.

THE next day the greatest excitement prevailed. The celebrated brigand, Bousian, had been caught, together with a large number of his band; the whole being incarcerated in the prison of Mostaganem. This Bousian had been for a long time the terror of the neighbourhood. He was tried and condemned some years ago, but succeeded in escaping from prison. He was then condemned to death *in contumaciam.* For several years the police have been on his track, but he has always managed to elude them. His feats at rapid movement were so great that some poor folks believed him to be a myth, and nursery-maids would turn him to account, to tranquillize refractory children. At last, however, he had been caught; and hence all this stir. We did not expect to see him, as the orders were to admit no one, except on business. However, our kind friend, the Administrator, introduced us to the public Prosecutor, who not only gave the necessary permission, but himself accompanied us.

At the prison, we were led past the sentries, to a court; at the end of which was a massive door with a small iron grating in the middle. On this being thrown open, Bousian was discovered sitting at the farther end, his ankles fastened together by an iron bar. He was short of stature, wore a Fez cap and the usual Arab dress. His look was one which I shall not easily forget; the only thing I have ever seen like it was a picture of Fagan in the condemned cell. When he saw us, he put on a careless, indifferent air; and once, in the course of conversation, actually smiled. He complained of the irons hurting his feet, and begged that they might be removed; but this could not be accorded. He asked for tobacco, and was told that some would be sent him. One of the party said, "If you had caught me on the other side of the Dahra, you would have cut my throat." Upon this being put into Arabic, he denied ever having taken life. Several assassinations are however laid to his charge, and the general belief is that he will be executed. I asked the public Prosecutor how long he thought it would take, before the case was concluded. He said several months, as the witnesses had to be fetched from a distance, and the charges were somewhat complicated.

After leaving Bousian, we went to see his lieutenant, who was confined in another part of the building, and to whom rumour accords the greater guilt of the two. He was a tall, thin, sallow man, of about four-and-twenty, with good features, and an intelligent countenance. He looked very ill, which appearance was put down to fear. He wore no irons; and upon our entry stood up and shook hands, kissing his hand after each salute, according to Arab fashion. Beside him stood a short, jovial-looking little Arab, who seemed delighted with everything and everybody. "Bon jour, tout le monde," was the salution he gave us. We thought, of course, that his crime was of the most venial character.

"What are you here for, my friend?"

"I killed my sister," was the cool reply.

"But what did you do that for?"

"Oh, I don't know; c'est une bêtise que j'ai faite."

Leaving these greater criminals, we passed into a room where about fifty prisoners were awaiting the assizes. On the entrance of the public Prosecutor, they all surrounded him; some thrust slips of paper into his hand, whilst others wished to carry on a verbal conversation. He made a few short replies, and then withdrew. We followed, and the door was locked, when it was found that one of our party had been locked in. This little incident caused a hearty laugh all round.

Our time for leaving Mostaganem was now drawing nigh. The best of friends must part; and we had now to bid adieu to the Administrator, a man whose courtesy and genial bearing make him beloved by rich and poor alike. He has already risen to a high position for so young a man, and will, no doubt, in the future fill one of the chief places in the colony. If any favour is shown to him in his career, owing to the great esteem in which his late father was held, I feel confident it could not be better placed.

On our way back to Relizane, we travelled with two priests. Fever, the curse of this country, had left its impress on the features of one. He said he was so weak at times that he could not hold a cup of coffee. This dreadful malady is remittent, and although it does not generally kill, it reduces its victims to such a state that many of them die from exhaustion; while others return to their native land, to live perhaps, but seldom to recover the vigour of perfect health.

At Relizane we took the train for Algiers. A young Arab, after wanting to carry our wraps, or do anything else in his power, asked for money. We gave him a sou, although he had done nothing. His eyes lighted up with joy, and as the train was moving off, we saw him kissing the coin in an ecstasy of delight.

The country presents an uninteresting aspect for some way, parts of the embankment of the railway are lined with a pretty tree or shrub, with a red flower (croton oil?). The guard wanted, to know if we meant to dine at Affreville, as it is the custom to telegraph in advance the number that may be expected. We were now in the province of Algiers, and a marked improvement was noticeable in the appearance of the country. Besides being much more fertile, it was more mountainous, and presented an agreeable change from the flat country through which we had lately been travelling. There were several villages of recent creation, all built on the same model —the *mairie*, the church, and the school being invariably the most conspicuous objects. Some of these will no doubt, in due course, rise to importance.

Orleansville is buried in trees, and looks very pretty; it has a garrison, and is now supplied with good water.

Affreville is close to the picturesque town of Miliana. We regretted that we had not decided to stop at the latter, as it is both historically interesting and beautifully situated. From here to Blidah, darkness prevented our seeing much.

At the station of La Chiffa, an Arab and his wife entered the carriage. The lady wore a thin white veil over the lower part of her face, concealing everything from the nose downwards, thus differing from the women of Oran, who content themselves with hiding their faces with their blankets.

This veil must in some measure interfere with the process of respiration, and cause great annoyance to the wearer in the sultry summer months, when breathing is difficult even under the most favourable circumstances. We had now been travelling for some sixteen hours, and were by no means sorry to leave the train, and deposit ourselves in the Hotel Geronde, at Blidah.

The next morning showed this to be an enchanting place, combining Alpine scenery and luxuriant southern vegetation. It must be seen after Spain and Oran, to be thoroughly appreciated. The gardens are among the most highly cultivated in Algeria; oranges and lemons abound, the papyrus flourishes, and the roads are fragrant with the scent of innumerable flowers and shrubs. Blidah is the head-quarters of the Algerian cavalry; and some remarkably fine horses are to be found in its stables.

The great excursion from here is to the Gorge of the Chiffa, which includes the Vallée des Singes. Leaving Blidah at

7 a.m., the *diligence* first goes to the Chiffa railway station, where the conductor hopes to pick up passengers from Algiers. It then makes for the gorge—the scenery becoming grander as the mountains close in. At half-past 10, we were at the little inn, at the mouth of the apes' valley. Here we breakfasted *à la fourchette;* and then began to search for monkeys. The first we saw was chained to its kennel. He—or rather she—for it was a female, notwithstanding its whiskers—had been captured some days before. She was very affable to the ladies; but upon seeing me, made evident signs of distaste, showing her teeth, and holding up her fist: this was because she had been caught by a man whose hat resembled mine. We left the little captive, and started up the valley. Soon a monkey was descried upon the opposite side; then another; then a large one carrying a little one on its back; then another and another, until we had counted some twenty or thirty of all sizes. An Arab boy who accompanied

us warned us not to approach too near, as the monkeys were apt to resent this liberty by a shower of stones. Had they been in a hollow, we might by a dexterous swoop have taken their positions without running much risk of a broken head; but as they occupied an eminence, we determined to leave them in undisturbed possession of their stronghold. Geraniums and roses grow plentifully in this valley; and before we returned to the inn, the ladies provided themselves with bouquets.

Hard by, is a small stalactite cave. The penalty of getting wet through has to be paid by those who venture in, the dripping from the rocks equalling a heavy torrent of rain. The cave is small; and, for those who have seen better, *le jeu ne vaut pas la chandelle.*

A four miles' walk, on a good road, gently ascending, brought us to the other end of the gorge; where we awaited the arrival of the evening coach to Medeah. This is a town whose elevation of 3,000 ft. commands for it a cool healthy climate, and from its immediate vicinity may be obtained extensive views over hill and dale. One day was sufficient to see it; so, passing again through the Gorge of the Chiffa, we returned to Blidah.

From here to Algiers is no great distance. The railway passes through a flat country, and nears the shores of the Mediterranean before the capital is reached. The station is close to the quay; and to enter even the modern town, pedestrians ascend long flights of steps.

CHAPTER XIV.

ALGIERS.

Invalids—Old and New Town—The Mosques—A Saint's Tomb—All Saints' Day—The Theatre—An Algerian Bath—Environs of Algiers—Service for the Drowned.

THE capital of Algeria is situated in about latitude 37° north, and longitude about 3° east. Its climate has the disadvantage of being too hot in summer and too cold in winter; the best months are probably April and November. It is resorted to in winter by delicate and consumptive patients, who arrive, for the most part, imagining that they are to have a cloudless sky and traditional May weather. Cold, rain, and wind soon drive away this fond delusion, and after the novelty of the place has worn off the invalid begins to pine for the bright glowing hearths of Old England. If his means and health will enable him to move elsewhere, well and good. But this is not always the case, when great efforts have been made and a home broken up, in order to bring one of its members to the so-called " sunny south:" the winter and the discomforts have to be borne ; and the family will perhaps consider themselves fortunate if a grave has not to be dug on the far-off African shore. In what I have said I do not wish to hinder those who, after careful consideration, have made up their minds to winter in Algiers, but I would advise such to remember that the average height of the thermometer is not the only thing to be thought of in illness. Cheerful society, English food, and home comforts are quite as necessary as a high temperature, and bright fires and freedom from draught a good deal more so. Few houses in the south of Europe and north of Africa have those appliances for keeping out cold which necessity has compelled us to adopt in England ; and everyone who has ever wintered on the Continent knows the difference between English hearths and the stove or the wood fire.

Begging the reader's pardon for this digression I return to Algiers, which consists of a new and an old town—the one being the creation of French art and architects, the other the ancient and historic city of the Deys. To give any idea of the latter to those who have not seen it, is a difficult task. The narrow tortuous streets, so steep that they have to be cut into steps to enable people to get up at all; the little square recesses which serve as shops, and in which it would be impossible for a man of ordinary stature to stand upright; the native *cafés*; here and there a mosque, or house of prayer; and above all, the strange and varied appearance of the inhabitants— Jews, Spaniards, Arabs, Maltese, etc., etc. —form a *tout ensemble* not easily to be imagined by stay-at-home folk.

The principal mosque—in a corner of which I saw a man lying fast asleep—

although a larger building, is, externally, not so fine as the new mosque, being quadrilateral in form, while the latter is in the shape of a cross. This latter is indeed the most imposing building in Algiers; it was founded in the seventeenth century, and, as aforesaid, resembles a cross, having been designed by a Christian architect, who suffered death for his audacity. The minaret attached to it contains a clock, which shows that such places are capable of being utilised for purposes other than calling the faithful to prayer.

We next visited one of the most remarkable tombs in Algeria, rendered specially attractive by its antiquity, as well as by the saintliness of Abd-er-Rahman, who there reposes. Shoes and boots had to be taken off on entering, but hats are a matter in which the convenience of the wearer is alone consulted. The tomb is hung with different coloured draperies, and surrounded with the usual votive offerings, of which ostrich eggs always form a part.

After having thoroughly examined this costly shrine, we pulled on our boots, the custodian accepting a gratuity which, if it did not go into his own pocket, was probably applied to the lighting and keeping clean of the chapel.

The Feast of All Saints coming off during our stay in Algiers, I went to the cathedral, which occupies the site of a mosque, and contains a good deal of its material. The mixed style of architecture in which these churches are built is almost entirely peculiar to this colony, if we except the Anglican Cathedral at Gibraltar. It is a kind of mixture of Moorish and Gothic, and is, of course, condemned in unqualified language by the red-tapists of architecture; but to unpretending amateurs like myself it has rather a pleasing effect—no doubt owing to want of taste.

A procession from the Archiepiscopal Palace to the cathedral attracted a goodly number of the heterogeneous population of Algiers, and must have caused considerable surprise to any Arabs who were seeing it for the first time. The archbishop, who celebrated, wore the usual pontifical vestments, and in procession carried his crozier in his left hand, using it as a walking-stick. A prodigious moustache, beard, and whiskers, prevented him from looking very priestly, but it gave him the air of a man; and I feel sure that his clergy, with their hair growing naturally on their faces, command quite as much respect as their slippery Italian and Spanish brethren. After the gospel his Grace delivered a discourse on the approaching Festival of All Souls, the effect of which was to send many of the weaker sex into tears.

In the afternoon a procession to the cemeteries was organised, and passed through the town, causing quite a little sensation to the Arab population.

The city contains a theatre, where operas and plays were being alternately performed. The music was not first rate; and the same might be said of the acting.

The old saying of "When in Turkey, do as the Turkeys do," took such hold upon me that I actually went to take an Algerian bath. After undressing, I was turned into an artificially heated room, with several Arabs, and there left for a quarter of an hour, to follow my own devices; after which I was pulled and pinched, and generally maltreated by the attendant—this did duty for shampooing. Subsequently, I was taken back to the place from whence I came, and given a cup of scented tea—I suppose as a kind of salve for the injuries that had just been inflicted. After getting a little cool, I began to untwist the turban and the winding-sheets in which I had been enveloped, and dressing, departed; determining that next time I wanted a bath, I would patronise a Christian establishment.

As to the environs of the town, many of them are very pretty; and are much frequented during the winter by the English, who live in villas which are let to the French during the summer, at much reduced rates. The suburb of Mustafa Supérieur is the most aristocratic; it is situated on the slope of a hill, and contains numerous houses in the French and Moorish styles.

Leaving the town on the western side, a very pretty walk leads to the curious church of Notre Dame d'Afrique, which is thoroughly Oriental in appearance, and very effective, owing both to its architecture and its elevated position. Every Sunday the clergy of this church perform the obsequies of all who may have been drowned in the Mediterranean during the previous week. After evening service, they proceed to the brow of the hill over-looking the sea, and there chant the Office for the Dead.

There are many other excursions to be made in the environs; but I must conclude this short notice of Algiers and its vicinity; recommending all who wish for farther information as to temperature, doctors, or the English church, to consult Mr. Murray's valuable Hand-book on Algeria; where, no doubt, all such information is duly stored.

CHAPTER XV.

BOUGIE TO SETIF.

Bougie—Its Historic Interest—Natural Features—"Bougies" —A Journey in the Diligence—Another Koubba—Gorge of Chabet-El-Akhira—Kabylia—Mount Babor—Setif—Diligence Arrangements.

ON Tuesday night, the 2nd of November, we were bidding adieu to the lights of Algiers, from the deck of one of the steamers of the "*Navigation Mixte*," bending its way towards Cape Matifou.

Of Dellys and its beauties—if it has any —we saw nothing, passing it in the middle of the night, and soon after dawn entering the harbour of Bougie. The view, always fine, was much enhanced by the clear atmosphere of the early morning, sharply defining the mountains as they rose from the sea, clothed with luxuriant verdure.

The historic interest of Bougie equals its natural beauties. It has been successively occupied by all the races which have overrun Northern Africa. It was at one time in the possession of Ferdinànd the Catholic of Spain; and then, great was its prosperity. Charles V., when defeated by the Moors, took refuge here, and subsequently abandoned it to his African conquerors. After this, the city gradually decayed, until taken by the French in 1833.

So much for its past. Its temples, palaces, churches may have disappeared, but its physical features ever remain; and looking across its bay, put me forcibly in mind of the view of the Estrelles from Cannes. The immediate neighbourhood affords shelter for the ,panther and the hyena; the latter may often be heard at night, prowling round the old town walls.

It has been said that the *bougies*, which so often form a point of disagreement between landlord and traveller, when figuring in a continental hotel bill, were originally made here; but none of the inhabitants seem to have any recollection of this, and all agree that no establishment for the manufacture of candles exists at present. What is more satisfactory still, is that no charge is made for the use of them, *bougies* being always, in Algeria, included in the price of the room.

As our time was limited, we could not spend more than one day in this reputed origin of so much light and so many disputes. So, taking the vehicle which by courtesy was called a *diligence*, we left at 4 a.m. the next morning. This getting up at unearthly hours is most annoying, and detracts very much from the pleasure of travelling; but in countries where long distances have to be traversed before another town can be reached, and the condition of many of the roads has to be taken into account, there is no help for it, and the only thing to be done is to smile and bear it.

For the first two hours we jolted along in the dark; and our thoughts—if a half-sleepy consciousness drifting in a certain direction can be called thought—were as to whether we should or should not be attacked by the wild animals. Such things had happened before, and might happen again for all we knew to the contrary, and the night was just the time when such an occurrence was most probable. Even the exciting nature of our reveries did not do more than just keep us awake; and when the sun ought to have risen, and unfolded a scene of surpassing loveliness, we became alive to the fact that it was a cloudy day— nay more, a rainy day, for a Scotch drizzle soon commenced; and we were destined to see the finest scenery in Algeria through that veil which so often obscures the beauty of a Highland peak. It was long indeed since we had seen any rain; and if it had come at any other time it would have been both gratefully and rejoicingly received.

Now and then the mist lifted, and we saw the tops of the mountains and some of their pointed outlines. We had followed the coast for a considerable distance; and arriving at Cape Okar, were able to look back over the wooded country we had passed through. Near at hand is the tomb of another Arab saint. Murray says of its occupant, that he was a man of such eminent holiness, that whenever he prayed the Marabouts of all other countries flocked round him, in the form of birds, to hear but the sound of his voice.

We turned inland, and soon entered the Gorge of Chabet-El-Akhira. It is not unlike the Gorge of the Chiffa, on rather a grander scale. Anyone who has seen several of these freaks of Nature cannot help being struck with the great similarity which they bear one to another. There is always the roaring torrent winding its way down the centre; now flowing with impetuous haste over rocks and shingle; now descending in a succession of semi-waterfalls; and then again broadening out, and for a time flowing peacefully along, as if wearied out with its previous exertions.

The road is blasted in many places in the side of the precipitous rock, showing that man has achieved some of his greatest triumphs side by side with Nature in her most majestic mood. The scene is sublime, grand, awful. This gorge is about five miles long; in passing through it we encountered nothing fiercer than a few monkeys.

At Kharata, according to French ideas, we breakfasted, although it was past eleven; but as we had eaten nothing that morning, except a few grapes and some dry bread, we were not particular as to what name the meal went by. Two bright-eyed maidens came in with things to sell, and were unveiled; for we were now in Kabylia, and that wretched custom of concealing the face is not practised in this mountainous district. The Kabyles are a distinct race from the Arabs; have different institutions, different laws, and a different language. The study of these people and their origin would no doubt afford as interesting a field for the speculations of anthropologists as the dwellers in the Basque provinces of Spain have already done.

The insurrection of 1871 originated in, and was chiefly confined to, this district. It would no doubt have been quickly suppressed, had not the troubles of France compelled her to withdraw her troops. When the communist rising was over, the army of Algiers was again re-inforced, and peace restored.

The huge Mount Babor, with its double peak, over 6,000 feet high, is a prominent object, and will one day become a favourite ascent—that is, when Algeria takes the place of Switzerland. Year by year tourists, tiring of their old haunts, seek out fresh ones; and there is no reason why these hitherto almost unknown regions should not become the head-quarters of an Atlas club, whose members will vie with each other in outstripping the energy and the zeal—not to say the foolhardiness—of their Alpine brethren.

We were now on high table-land, and the weather was intensely cold; the roads

—if such they might be called—execrable; and our cart—it could hardly be called by any other name—such that the rain and wind penetrated through it, and wet us nearly to the skin. When we reached Setif, at eight o'clock that evening, we were feeling so miserable that if a wish could have transported me back to London I would have eschewed travelling for the rest of my life. However, a fair dinner and a good night's rest made us all take a more favourable view of affairs.

If anyone came here with the idea of sight-seeing, he would be grievously disappointed; for, putting aside the usual Arab costumes, with which we had now become familiarized, there was absolutely nothing worthy of notice. The town, as it stands, is almost entirely French, and is situated in an immense plain, with hardly a hillock in any direction. Once outside the walls, the eye wanders over a treeless track of country, and finds nothing to break the outline of the horizon.

The minaret of the mosque is perhaps the best feature in Setif. The interior of that building is small, and in the usual style. The weather was cold and exhilarating, owing to the altitude of these table-lands —from 3,000 to 4,000 feet above sea level. Those who have been for years or months in hot or tropical countries know the intense pleasure with which the first cold weather is always welcomed. The body seems invigorated, and exertion, instead of being as hitherto, a painful effort, becomes a pleasure.

The hours of starting for the *diligences* here almost rival those of Spanish trains in their inconvenience and total disregard for public comfort. The two for Constantine both start in the evening, and arrive there the following morning, thus depriving one of a night's rest; for who can sleep when jolted along in one of these ill-conditioned vehicles? In summer no doubt the arrangement has its advantages, for the days are too hot for travelling; but with the thermometer barely above freezing it is inexplicable.

CHAPTER XVI.

CONSTANTINE.

Constantine—Its Situation and Associations—Public Buildings—Batna—Lambessa—Ancient Inscriptions.

CONSTANTINE—situated about forty miles inland—capital of one of the provinces into which Algeria is divided—containing a population of 30,000, is the most remarkable city in the colony. None other of the large towns has so well conserved its Mahomedan manners and customs, and none other has so magnificent a position. To the tourist, few places can offer more interest—even Algiers is thrown into the shade, when compared with it; and Toledo —surrounded by its deep ravine—is eclipsed by the perpendicular cliffs which form the natural defences of this city, and which are in many places sheer precipices of 1,000 feet. From the town itself they would be almost unobserved; it is only when the traveller walks round the walls that he can fully appreciate what Nature has done for the defences of Constantine.

From its earliest history it has been the envy and desire of those who did not possess it. Its troubles began long before the Christian era, and continued until it was taken by storm, on the 13th of October, 1837, when its last Bey fled before the victorious French. Hadj Ahmed had defeated them only a year previously, and on this occasion made a brave defence, but all to no avail. The lover of Church History may remember that the struggles between Donatist and Catholic once swayed the popular mind here; until both alike perished before the invading Arab.

The architect will find the palace and the mosques as fine as any in the colony; and the antiquarian may yet discover some traces of these bygone times, although unhappily they are fast disappearing before so-called French improvements. Lions, panthers, hyenas, foxes, all exist within fifty miles of the city; not in the tame condition in which they are seen in Regent's park, but in his wild native grandeur the king of beasts disports himself in these mountains.

In my first walk through Constantine, it reminded me more of Tangier than anything in Algeria, the proportion of Arabs being much larger than that at Algiers or Oran. The Grand Mosque is believed to have been built over the remains of a pagan temple. It stands in a conspicuous position, in a broad street. The richness of the marbles and colouring of the mosque of Salah Bey surpasses anything of the kind in Algeria. Entering it by a flight of marble steps, through an iron gate a court is reached, the middle of which is filled with trees and shrubs rising from a lower level. A carved door admits to the mosque, and it is there that its splendour becomes evident; the *mihrab* and the *mimbar* (the former the recess towards which Mahomedans pray, the latter the pulpit) are particularly fine.

The cathedral is also an ancient mosque, built in the pleasing Arabesque style; it contains some marbles and a handsome pulpit. On Sunday high mass was celebrated soon after 9 a.m. I looked in vain among the congregation for fellow-males; women there were in plenty, but not a single man was to be seen. Speaking on the subject afterwards to a gentleman in the local administration, he said that Freethinking was more advanced in Algeria than in France, and that it was quite the exception for men to attend mass.

The palace of Hadj Ahmed, the last Bey, is much praised by some writers; but I think, hardly deserves all the encomiums which they have lavished upon it. Lately it has come down in the world, having been turned into public offices, and a residence for the chief military authorities.

There is a remarkable bridge called El

Kantara, which crosses the gorge, several hundred feet deep, to the Kasba. This bridge is a favourite place for Arabs who are wearied with the toil and suffering of the present life, to throw themselves over. A painful incident of this kind happened the morning of our arrival, when a man—by accident or design—fell, and was dashed to pieces in the depths below.

The night of the 9th of November, the coach (they *will* start in the evening) conveyed us across the bridge, *en route* for Batna. The air was cold, as we were still on the great table-land, which is the natural division between the Tell (a small fertile slip along the coast), and the Sahara. The moon shone out brightly, as we jolted merrily along a good road; the changing of horses serving to break the monotony of the journey, as well as the sleep of the passengers. At 7 a.m. we were in Batna, having travelled some eighty miles in the course of the night. This town is situated 4,000 feet above the sea, and almost due south of Constantine, being the half-way house between it and the Desert. The cold was intense, and I had recourse to jumping, and violent swinging about of arms, in order to keep the circulation going.

The next day we took a small carriage, and drove to Lambessa, about seven miles distant; and having called upon a gentleman to whom we had a letter of introduction, went in search of the ruins of this once important Roman town, which reached its zenith about the third or fourth century. Within the Prætorium—the principal building still extant—is a collection of the antiquities found in the neighbourhood. The most interesting are the Christian and pagan inscriptions. Some begin "Deo," showing the Christian belief in the unity of God; others have Greek crosses at the commencement, or between two words towards the close. I looked in vain for the Latin cross; it was nowhere to be seen. In the catacombs in Rome I have noticed much the same thing; only *there*, the lower part is sometimes slightly elongated, having the appearance of being in a state of transition. From this, I am inclined to believe that the Greek form was the ancient Christian symbol, and the Latin a more modern development. There were some letters other than the Roman; one resembled a Greek upsilon; another I was unable to classify.

It is a pity that so little of this once flourishing town remains. Great portions of it have been taken to build the neighbouring houses. Some of our party went to the remains of a temple, but did not describe it as anything very remarkable. To be a large convict establishment, is the present fate of Lambessa. Close to the building used for this purpose a very interesting pavement has been found, which is now carefully preserved.

On our way back we were told that lions were formerly very numerous; and that, not long since, a lady and gentleman driving home one night were set upon by one, who devoured the horse; while they, in the greatest terror, were expecting their turn to come next. The darkness was great; but there was nothing to be done but to wait till his majesty had finished his supper; when, luckily for them, he took himself off. No such adventure happened to us, I am sorry to say; otherwise, I should have been much pleased to give a thrilling and graphic description of the whole affair; not forgetting to mention the deeds of fame which each had accomplished when in the presence of the monster.

We retired early to rest that night, for at four o'clock next morning we were to start for the Sahara; and hoped, if everything went right, to reach the oasis of Biskra at eight o'clock the same evening.

CHAPTER XVII.

THE DESERT.

The Van—"The Golden Gate of the Desert"—First Sight of the Sahara—The Ziban—Biskra—Sidi-Okba—Native Attentions—Mahomedan Saints—Desert Sunsets—A Café of the Oasis—Funeral Rites—Venomous Reptiles—Return to Batna.

It was hardly worth going to bed, for at three o'clock we began to stir, and when at a quarter to four we turned out into the bleak cold night, our general appearance was anything but cheerful. A tumble-down looking van was shown us as the vehicle in which we had engaged our places for Biskra, and when we were seated, it was discovered that one of the windows would not shut, so we had fresh morning air with a vengeance. After leaving Batna the road ascends, having a large forest at some distance on the right. In a few hours the highest point is reached, and the descent commences, vegetation becoming scanty, or having almost entirely disappeared. We met a number of caravans coming north with dates. Very picturesque indeed was the appearance of these sons of the desert, with their wives and their camels, and it was the only thing which relieved the tediousness of the journey, until, at about eleven o'clock, we came upon the northern side of the oasis of El Kantara. The little inn nestling among its fruit trees was what our Transatlantic cousins would have called " a sight good for sore eyes," and eyes were very likely to be sore after gazing so long at the desolate waste through which we had been descending. The southern slopes of the Atlas vie with the Castilles in barrenness; facing full south, they are equally exposed to the burning rays of the mid-day sun, and—to what is far worse—the scorching sirocco. Only where flows that life-giving fluid, water, is this country fertile;

and there springs up one of these oases, the joy of man and beast.

El Kantara has been described as "the golden gate of the desert." It consists of a northern and a southern part, connected by a very remarkable gorge. At the former, we breakfasted; and afterwards strolled amongst the cool green vegetation, surrounded by the fruit-trees of Old England. Then passing through the deep, narrow defile, we came upon a waving sea of green, in which lay thousands and thousands of the rich date-palm. I have often seen this tree cultivated on the shores of the Mediterranean, but only in his native clime and under a tropical sun does this majestic king of the desert attain to the full magnificence of his stately growth. The temperature was appreciably higher than when we entered the gorge; and a few mud huts peeping from among the trees told of a different people.

El Kantara was soon left behind, and we were again driving along a dusty road, crossing here and there dry, or partially dry, water-courses. In spring, when swollen with the melting snow, these are quite impassable. The water eventually reaches the desert, where it either gets absorbed in the sand, or helps to fill those great salt lakes which constitute one of the chief features of this part of Africa. About sunset we ascended the last spur of the Atlas; and then saw for the first time the immense tracts of the Sahara stretching out before us, as far as the eye could reach, black spots scattered here and there marking the different oases of the Ziban. The one for which we were bound was happily the nearest, and at eight our journey was ended. Sixteen hours is a long time to pass in a van; but to sleep in an oasis of the desert is a pleasure which must be paid for in some shape or other.

The Ziban country consists of a group of oases lying between the thirty-fourth and thirty-fifth degrees of north latitude, and the fifth and seventh of east longitude. Biskra, taken by the French, some thirty years since, and now a military depôt, is the capital. It is the last point in this direction in which European soldiers are to be found, and those stationed here have generally misconducted themselves elsewhere. Formerly, there was a small garrison at Tuggurt, but the climate was found to be so unhealthy that it was withdrawn. It may therefore be considered that the French supremacy virtually ends here, although the frontier is supposed to be some degrees farther south, and taxes are exacted from the chiefs of the different oases. The question as to the southern boundary of Algeria has always been a delicate one. I believe the latest idea is to make it coincide with the thirty-second parallel of latitude, thus including El Goleah.

Those who have not seen an oasis can have but little idea of its exquisite beauty. To walk among the palm groves, to listen to the stream as it trickles peacefully by, and breathe in the balmy air—is like a taste of fairy-land. These oases must be to the desert what the islands are to the South Pacific—the bright spots with which this world is here and there studded.

We made an excursion to Sidi Okba, distant some fourteen miles to the south. There is nothing but sand and small loose stones to be seen on the way. The road—if such it may be called—was execrable; we often had to get out and walk, and the carriage was several times nearly overturned. A dark purple ridge against the horizon gradually changed as we approached it into the shady green of the numberless palms of which the oasis is composed, the little mud village lying buried amongst these trees.

We had intended to breakfast at the chief's house, and had provided ourselves with the usual present, a coloured tumbler; but unhappily this functionary had gone to another village, to lament the death of a nephew; so the coloured tumbler is still in my possession. We entered a hut, supported in the interior by mud pillars, and roofed with palm leaves, where we asked to have some eggs cooked. The arrival of Europeans, and especially of European ladies, is an event in Sidi`Okba not soon to be forgotten. Wherever we went we were accompanied by the whole juvenile population of the village, and now that we were in a hut, they crowded round the door, and stared at us as if we had been live kangaroos. Our host, thinking that these attentions must be unwelcome, made a sudden dash at the door—or rather opening, for there was no door—and dispersed the crowd. No sooner had he returned to superintend the cooking of the eggs, than the doorway was again filled by curious and eager spectators. He then hit upon a new expedient —filling a jug with water, he dashed it over the unsuspecting mob. This caused a temporary flight; but two minutes was quite sufficient to allay the panic, and the entrance was once more besieged by our admirers. Water was again brought into requisition; and we were kept amused in this way until our breakfast was ready.

I now came to the conclusion that the great anxiety was to see us eat. No doubt these simple people thought we had some new and strange method of conveying the food to our mouths, and were, I daresay, actuated by much the same feeling which induces some of us to pay the extra sixpence to see the animals fed at a menagerie. A few privileged Arabs were allowed to enter, and seated themselves cross-legged at a respectful distance. A Marabout, or Arab saint, on account of his sanctity, was permitted to take up a reserved position, immediately in front of the ladies; and so the breakfast began. Bread, hard-boiled eggs, and wine, made up our frugal meal. The holy man in front, looking as if he too would like something, we gave him an egg. He ate it with avidity, and put me very much in mind of a monkey performing the same task. I offered him a cigarette, which he began to eat with the same relish; until a kind friend pointed out that it was intended for another purpose.

Saints in Barbary are of three descriptions—those who are saints by descent, those who have made the pilgrimage to Mecca, and those who are saints through their eccentricities. These latter would, in other countries, pass under the name of fools, or persons slightly deranged; but unsophisticated people like the Arabs look upon a visitation of this kind as a special testimony of Divine Grace; and so the Marabout is allowed to do what he likes and go where he will, having a claim for support upon all true believers.

Our breakfast ended, we emerged from our den, to the great delight of the Sidi Okbians, who had gathered in crowds, awaiting this event. The ladies' blue veils and fans excited the greatest amount of surprise; some of the children, bolder than the rest, would come up and touch some part of their dress, and then run away, as if they were afraid that we should turn round and snap.

The mosque contains the tomb of the saint whose name the oasis bears. As Sidi Okba died in the seventh century, this is sometimes considered the most ancient Mahomedan building in Africa.

The interest which our arrival had excited, did not abate as time wore on; and it was only when we entered a private palm-grove that we were alone. The proprietor drove out the crowd, and then came with his wife and children, to present us with dates. The women and girls all wear an abundance of immense ear-rings, tattoo their persons, and colour their teeth and nails. They were not veiled; happily for them, the desert too is free from a custom which, one would think, must lead to suffocation in summer.

The time for our departure had arrived, and we returned to Biskra by the same road. The sun sets here with unusual splendour; immediately he has sunk below the horizon, all colour seems to vanish; but in twenty minutes or half-an-hour, returns that brilliant after-glow which is the pride of the south.

> "Not as in northern climes, obscurely bright,
> But one unclouded blaze of living light."
> > BYRON.

There is not much to be done in the desert, after sunset, unless one goes to the native *café;* so thither I repaired. It was well-lighted and well-filled. The musicians consisted of one man with a drum, and another with a wind instrument, the sound of which resembled a bagpipe. The latter, in order to bring himself and his atrocious machine into prominence, stood upon a bench, swayed his body backwards and forwards, and blew as if for his life. This, assisted by the drum, produced a noise which was almost deafening. A damsel in full desert dress came in, and went through her dance. The feet and head move but slightly, but the body is kept shaking, as if the performer were afflicted by the palsy. The dance is anything but elegant, and would not take if put on the English stage. When she had finished, other girls came in, and did likewise. This is the amusement to which the desert Arab looks forward, when his toils are finished, and he shall have safely arrived in Biskra.

Leaving the noise and smoke, I took a turn among the gardens, lighted by the full moon, and then went to the edge of the oasis. Here I saw a little fellow, who, though boasting of no covering, performed somersaults in hopes of gaining a few pence. The lugubrious sound of " Oh! oh! oh! oh! " caught my ear in the distance, and I went in the direction. A large concourse of people, chiefly women, were gathered in a circle, making the sounds referred to. They mingled this with every external show of grief. I soon learned that some notable had died, and that the mourning would go on for a fortnight. As I lay in my bed that night, I could hear nothing but groaning, lamentation, and woe, for the mourners were not three hundred yards off.

A very fine garden belonging to a private gentleman, formed our next day's excursion.

It is beautifully kept, and contains a great variety of tropical plants.

It would be a mistake to go away with the idea that the desert has no drawbacks. I have just seen a large glass bottle of spirits of ammonia, containing several varieties of the delightful reptiles which abound in the oases. They had been two years in bottle, and, like wine, become more valuable the longer they are kept—at least the spirit which contains them does. The colonists say that the ammonia, being permeated with the essence of these venomous creatures, is a perfect cure when applied to the bite of one of the same species; thus verifying the old saying, "A hair out of the dog's tail that bit you;" as also the homœopathic motto of "*similia similibus.*" The greatest danger is to be apprehended from the horned viper, (*Vipère à cornes*) which is very common, and whose bite is fatal (if no remedies be taken) in about twenty minutes. In case of an accident, the usual method is instantly to use caustic, potash or ammonia (a phial of which should always be at hand), taking care that it penetrates to the deepest part of the wound. Another way—probably more effectual, but requiring greater courage in the application—is to burn the part with a red hot iron, or to cut it out with an ordinary penknife. I saw a specimen of this snake in the bottle mentioned; it was a young one, hardly a foot long, of a light grey colour, having two horns on its head, resembling those of the garden snail, only much bigger. Tarantulas and scorpions are very frequently met with, in the houses; one of the latter was killed this morning in the room next to mine. Their bite, although producing unpleasant consequences, seldom, if ever, proves fatal. I was told that a large snake, which my informant called a Boa-constrictor, had recently made his appearance in one of the lower oases, and amused himself by carrying off native children whenever he had a mind or an appetite. If true, it must make that part of the country rather a convenient neighbourhood for large families and small means.

We visited some of the neighbouring villages, and found in them all, the same mud huts of one story, the same inquisitive people, and the same date-palms spreading their luxuriant foliage over the same peacefully trickling streams. The desert is a country of winds; and Biskra is fully exposed, except to the sea-breezes, from which it is protected by the mountains. The evidence of high winds can be seen in some of the palms, which are much bent; their motto should be, " *Flecti non frangi.*"

The next morning, we were to leave at two; so instead of going to bed, we spent the night in walking about, in order to be ready. The desert looked its best, for a full moon shone vertically down. I was sorry when eighteen hours of travelling over the same route brought us back to the cold, bleak, Alpine region of Batna—sorry when we saw for the last time the waving palms of El Kantara—sorry when we bade adieu to the people, their mud huts, and their glorious sunsets. But every cloud has its silver lining—there were no flies to bully one's life out here, and the same could hardly be said of Biskra.

I cannot quit the desert altogether, without saying a word upon the scheme recently started for flooding portions of this vast area of country by letting in the Mediterranean. A large part of the Sahara is stated to be below the surface of the sea, and as it is a very well established truth that water has a partiality for the lowest practicable level, there is not the slightest doubt that if the present obstructions which divide the two could be removed, the Mediterranean might be induced to part with a few million gallons of water in favour of its more sandy rival. The barriers to this union are not so very great in some parts of Tunis. Near Gabes are large salt lakes: by making two or three small cuttings it is very possible that these lakes might be brought in contact with the Chott Melghir (south of

Biskra), and this latter might be turned into a depôt from which to water the rest of the country. It is in fact highly probable that all these salt lakes were formerly one vast sheet of water, of whose extent it is difficult now even to guess. Roman remains are said to have been discovered in Ghadamis, and it is scarcely possible that even an enterprising people like the Romans could have penetrated to such a distant place unless they had had some facilities other than those known to us.

The consternation which the sudden arrival of the sea in front of a distant oasis would cause among the inhabitants, is not easily to be imagined. The smaller reptiles would first suffer, and hard times it would be for those in whose early education swimming had not formed a prominent part. Mud huts would disappear, while antelopes took to their heels; even an ostrich, considering the extreme exigencies of the case, might be induced to try his hand at a fly.

If the plan be adopted I cannot see how

it can be carried out without great loss to life and property; but perhaps its promoters may know of some means by which all this can be avoided; and we may yet live to see the "Ocean of Sahara." Locomotion from one island oasis to another will then be comparatively easy, instead of as at present the most difficult travelling in the world, excepting the Arctic and Antarctic regions.

From Biskra to Tuggurt a horse may be taken, but to penetrate beyond that latter place the camel is the only available animal. He who wishes to go on in spite of all difficulties, and who cannot afford to equip an expedition at his own cost, should engage the services of one or two of these beasts, make a stipulation with the chief of a caravan to be allowed to join his party, take plenty of water, firearms, and trinkets, make his will, and then trust to Providence.

CHAPTER XVIII.

BATNA TO TUNIS.

The Aïssaoui—Philippeville—Bona—S. Augustine—Separation—Disembarkation at La Calle—Goletta—The Lake.

A TEDIOUS night's journey brought us back to Constantine, where we intended to spend a few days in resting. One evening, when dining with some friends, our host suggested that we should go and see the Aïssaoui— " a Mahomedan sect who, though not numerous, have certain religious observances which it is to be hoped," he said, " are confined to themselves. Their principal stronghold is Tunis; and their branches extend into the neighbouring countries. Every Friday evening, they have a service in their mosque. It consists in inflicting upon themselves and each other, the most excruciating tortures that the ingenuity of man can devise. Among other examples, may be taken," continued our host, " running themselves through with swords and other pointed instruments— burning themselves with hot irons—eating fire, glass, live scorpions and serpents—or in fact, anything else equally unpalatable and indigestible."

The ladies had no objection to go; and I, of course, was only too glad to see anything and everything that came in my way. Our host begged to be excused accompanying us, because he said the sight was so " *dégoûtant* " (I use his own word) that it made him ill for several days. He therefore sent his Arab servant to show us the way, and carry chairs for the ladies.

Some minutes before reaching the mosque, we could hear the noise and din within. When arrived at that revered spot, our guide took the ladies in, and put them in a place as much out of the way as possible. My first view on entering was of two Aïssaoui, one on each side, yelling, shrieking, foaming at the mouth, and looking as if they would like to spring upon and bite all visitors, if only the Arabs who held them would let them go. I quickly made for a corner; but no part of the building seemed safe. There was a man just in front of me flourishing about a red-hot poker; he had all the appearance of a maniac, and I should not have minded if he had moved a little farther off. I had only one eye to see what was going forward, as the other had to be devoted to the exclusive service of the gentleman with the poker. There seemed to be in the centre of the mosque, some twenty or thirty young men, with a cloth girt round their loins, and long hair flowing down their backs. When not engaged in any special act of torture, they swayed their bodies and beat time to the drums.

My friend with the poker, I was pleased to see, had been replaced by a man who was doing nothing worse than eating half a pane of glass.

I looked upon him quite complacently.

An Aïssaoui now came up with a pan filled with live coals. "I hope he does not mean to throw these over the company," I began to think, as I glanced round to see what openings there were for an escape.

He only wanted to eat them.

I was very pleased when I saw the last disappearing down his throat; and that source of anxiety removed.

No sooner had he finished (troubles never *will* cease) than two more Aïssaoui, who evidently acted in concert, came my way; one carried a sword, which he was no doubt going to stick into somebody, and the other a large hammer to ram it in, as soon as the first had fixed it.

Suspense again! Why does he not select his victim quickly?

Good gracious! He is actually looking at me; surely he cannot take me for an Aïssaoui—he must know I do not look like one—and if he only considered the objection I have to pointed instruments——

Just then I saw my old friend with the poker (which I expect he had been reheating) making for his former quarters. This was really more than one could be expected to stand; so, with a courage for which I give myself credit, I made a dash for the ladies' corner, and said hurriedly, although composedly,—

"Don't you think we had better be going? This is very '*dégoûtant.*'"

At this moment the music ceased.

The Aïssaoui, with their eyes starting out of their heads, and maddened with pain and excitement, rushed upon each other with the fury of wild beasts, giving utterance to sounds which—until I heard them there—I should have thought only brute animals could produce.

Watching an opportunity, we made for the doors. They were opened for an instant to let us through, and then speedily closed, "for," said the doorkeeper, "if any of those within were to get without in their present state, they might do mischief."

"Might!" I replied. "If you let that fellow with the poker loose, he will probably slaughter half the population."

When we returned to our friends our host smiled, and asked us coolly if we had enjoyed ourselves. We tried to look affable, and replied, "Very much;" although I should have liked to tell him what a narrow escape we had had, and how very reprehensible it was in him to allow us to enter such a den unarmed.

"Some of the customs are very singular," he went on.

("Uncommonly so," I thought.)

"It is strange that no one is ever killed, and that no blood is ever shed."

("If he had only mentioned that before," I thought to myself, "I should have been comparatively easy.")

"Do you think it is done by jugglery then?" I inquired.

"A great deal of it probably is," he said; "but I am inclined to think that a good deal of it is also genuine." And so the subject dropped.

The railway from Constantine to Philippeville descends considerably before reaching the sea, the country traversed being wild and mountainous. The latter place is entirely modern, and is the port of Constantine, for which purpose it was no doubt created. A beautiful road, hemmed in with luxuriant vegetation, where singing birds warble forth their little songs, leads to the village of Stora, about four miles distant; and there are fine views of the bay from several points.

Rough weather kept us at Philippeville two days. At last the steamer from Marseilles arrived, and we embarked for Bona, called, "La plus jolie ville de l'Afrique." It is certainly a pretty place, although hardly deserving so very high an epithet. It has a convenience which those who have been accustomed to landing in small boats will appreciate—a pier. One walks on board; and, for the first time since landing at Honfleur, I walked ashore.

Nothing could be seen that night, as we did not get in until past seven; but the next morning we looked round, and found a clean well-built town—Algerian in every particular. There are in the neighbourhood some very extensive iron mines, which yield an immense profit to those fortunate enough to have anything to do with them.

Half-an-hour's walk outside the town, brings the traveller to the ancient city of Hippo. Very little indeed remains of it. Here it was, however, that the blessed Augustine once ministered; and hence he gave to the world his celebrated confessions. An altar erected to his memory commemorates the scene of his labours. It is a beautiful spot, surrounded by a park-like country—very different from the bustling city which once occupied the ground. Christianity—after twelve hundred years of, one might almost say extinction—again begins to rise over its ancient ruins. Once more the cross is elevated, and the crescent wanes—such is the changing course of this world's events.

I here had to bid adieu to the two ladies

whom I had been permitted to accompany in our tour of Algeria, and in whose society I had passed so many pleasant hours. They were returning to Paris, but my work was not yet done. The Regency of Tunis was at hand, and its capital I was bound to see. After that, I too might bid adieu to Africa. We left Bona, and, with it, Algeria; they on the 25th, and I on the 27th, of November.

My steamer made for La Calle, the last town in the colony; but it was too rough to disembark the passengers, so they were carried on to Tunis. Night came on; and early the next morning, we had entered the gulf. The vessel stopped; then went on for a short distance; then stopped again; finally dropping anchor about a mile from the shore. Disembarkation—always a source of annoyance—had its usual evils greatly aggravated by the distance we were from the land; and also by there being no tariff, thus enabling the boatmen to demand whatever they please. A fellow-passenger said that, on one occasion, he had to pay forty francs for being rowed ashore, the excuse for so high a charge being, that the sea was rough. As a great many boats gathered round us, all eager for passengers—and as the sea had the good manners to behave itself,—we got off pretty easily; and in about half-an-hour were landed at Goletta, the port of Tunis.

The capital itself is situated on the other side of the large lake, on whose shores Goletta lies. A canal connects the lake with the sea, so that vessels can pass to and fro. A sail across, was the former means of reaching Tunis; but latterly, that development of the nineteenth century— the steam-engine—has penetrated even into the Regency, and a train now conveys passengers to the capital. The carriages are rather different from those used in other parts, having a verandah running along each side, for the whole length of the train, so that travellers can stroll up and down during the journey, and thus change the usual sitting posture. In countries where a railway passes through fine scenery, this mode should be adopted without delay. The line skirts the lake for nearly the whole way—some nine miles. Birds of many descriptions flew off at our approach; and the sportsman must here find an endless variety on which to exercise his gun.

CHAPTER XIX.

TUNIS.

Tunis—The Bey—The Streets—The People—Carthage—On Board—A Storm at Sea—Hammamet—Pantellaria—Dining under Difficulties—Sicily Reached.

THE view of Tunis from a distance is, like that of all Arab cities, very imposing; the whiteness of its buildings giving it a cleanly and inviting appearance. It is only when entered that this delusion is dispelled, and the true nature of the city revealed—grovelling in all its virgin filth. The station is in the European quarter, and outside the town. An unfinished appearance characterises this suburb—houses are seen half-built, and the dust which building always occasions is sure to find out the stranger's eyes.

Before giving a description of the town,

I should like to mention, for the benefit of those who have not their geography at their finger ends—that Tunis is the capital of a country in North Africa, bearing the same name; and that the chief officer in the administration is styled the Bey. He—like all his race—never fails in his duty of fine words and fair speeches. The Sultan of Turkey, to whom he owes allegiance, receives with the utmost regularity all the expressions of submission which His Highness considers it a privilege to be allowed to pay. But when it comes to handing over the tribute, a very different story has to be told; and the Porte may consider itself fortunate if it receive any money from Tunis, except at the investiture of a new Bey. When difficulties arise with foreign powers, His Highness generally settles the matter without any reference to the Porte; it is only when the question is peculiarly delicate or intricate, and when a direct answer might still farther complicate affairs, that he shields himself behind Constantinople, and refers the foreign representatives to that quarter.

The title of Bey is hereditary in his family; and on an accession a kind of religious investiture of the office is made by Turkey, which, according to usage, has to be heavily paid for. In other respects, this dignitary, once instituted, is perfectly independent, and is the absolute controller and proprietor of the lives and possessions of his subjects. His power knows no limit, and the only influence which tends to restrict its use—or perhaps I should rather say, abuse—is the presence of the foreign consuls. All these African despots know—or ought to know—that their chief prosperity comes from being on good terms with European powers, and the recollection of the fate which befell the late Dey of Algiers has probably had a salutary effect upon his brother tyrants.

The streets of Tunis are somewhat different from those of Algerian and Moorish towns, being covered in for much longer distances, presenting the appearance of a vast bazaar. Trade is carried on with a briskness surprising in an Oriental city; the manufacture of carpets and gold embroidery seems to take the chief place. The mosques are not accessible to any but the faithful, so what may be inside is a matter for conjecture. The principal one, approached by a flight of steps, is of considerable size. Beyond the streets and the people there is not much to be seen.

The palace where the Bey resides is at Bardo. I went there on a Monday, having been told that that was the day on which the sovereign personally administered justice. It was, however, on Saturdays that this was done, so I only saw portions of the palace, and made the acquaintance of the Bey's interpreter, who promised to accompany me to the Hall of Justice if I came next Saturday. As, however, the Palermo steamer left on Wednesday, I was unable to avail myself of the offer. The justice administered is often, I was told, of the most rudimentary character, and the expression on the faces of the unfortunate suitors, as they leave this highest court of final appeal, a painful sight to witness.

The usual dress for the ministers of State, and all persons wishing to be thought in *haute société*, as well as for the soldiers, is, excepting the Fez cap, entirely European. The common people retain the Arab costume. The Jewesses, unlike any I had previously seen, wear tight leggings and a tunic. A black veil is used by some of the Tunisian women to conceal their faces, otherwise there is nothing to distinguish them from the women of eastern Algeria.

On returning to Goletta, I saw a number of prisoners chained by bars, looking the picture of wretchedness; but, indeed, that was the general appearance of nearly everyone I met—some of the soldiers were quite pitiable to behold.

The remains of Carthage are within a walk of Goletta. I wandered about for some time, without seeing very much, except the Chapel of S. Louis. The individual whom this building commemorates was at one period of his life King of France. He went to fight in the Holy Wars, and returning from one of those campaigns, thought he would besiege Tunis, and in so doing, perished on the spot where his chapel now stands. The few ruins left of Carthage show how completely even the greatest cities can perish. Were it not for history and tradition, its very locality might be unknown.

I was much disappointed in the size and general appearance of the Palermo steamer, and had I not taken my passage, and had the difficulties of getting backwards and forwards to the land not been so great, I should have preferred going by way of Sardinia rather than remaining on board, when I discovered that I was to be the only first-class passenger, and that the captain, crew, and cabin boy—all told—only numbered thirteen hands.

On Thursday evening, the 2nd of December—the time subsequently fixed for departure—a south wind was blowing, and the captain decided not to put to sea: he knew best the capabilities of his bark. Friday evening, the wind having changed to the west, we began a voyage of which it can only be said that it is fortunate it ever had an end—or rather, a successful end. As long as we were in the Gulf of Tunis all went well, but this did not last. In a few hours I woke to a consciousness that there was unusually stormy weather, and at four in the morning three tremendous seas struck the ship with such violence that it seemed impossible that she could right herself. I got up and dressed hastily. The storm was raging, and the mingled sounds of wind, sea, and engines, the creaking of the vessel, and the smashing of crockery, produced an effect which to the non-sailor mind can only be called appalling. There is nothing like being cheerful under all circumstances, and if we are born to be drowned, nothing that we can do will obviate it; so lighting a long cigar, I sat down, awaiting the time when, all human efforts having failed, the captain should give the signal for prayers.

The blessed light of day broke at length: the two hours from four to six had seemed like ten. The sea had in no degree abated, and the light was really but of little service; and yet what a difference it made! By means of it the African coast could be perceived to the west, and as the wind came from that direction, we were doing our best to get close in where the water would naturally be smoother. By ten we managed to reach Hammamet, a small town in the Regency of Tunis, and there we lay in bad anchorage all Saturday. Nearly the whole of the crockery on board was broken; and one of the lamps hung in the saloon had been wrenched from its fastenings, and swung against the deck with such violence that the metal part was completely bent in. On Saturday evening the sun shone out for the first time that day, and Hammamet looked the better for it.

Sunday morning, the wind having somewhat moderated, we started, and hugging the slightly undulating coast nearly as far as Cape Bon, turned sharp west, and ran before the wind. The Italian island of Pantellaria came in sight just as the African coast was getting invisible. At one time we could see the two, Europe and Africa, but it was not for long. In the midst of the troubled waves lay the mountainous island still far away, looking—shall I say?—like an oasis in the desert. It came nearer and nearer, until we could see the houses, the animals grazing in the fields, the huge waves breaking against the rocky coast. We should get in by sunset, and there, I thought, should pass a quiet and undisturbed night on *terra firma;* for the sea and the wind were still uncomfortably high.

A signal from the shore, and my afternoon's dream was dispelled—it was too rough to land. Disappointments are hard to bear; and harder still it was to turn from the inviting land in the cold grey light, and face the storm, which had now assumed all the proportions of Friday night. We tried to dine, but it was under difficulties. The only way in which I could keep near the table, was by kneeling down and placing one arm round its leg. Sitting on a chair was quite out of the question in the present state of the weather, as the chair and its occupant would soon part company. One of those squalls for which the Mediterranean is famous, came on. The water dashed over the decks, and had not all the apertures leading to the engines been instantly closed, the fires would have been forthwith extinguished, and our condition rendered still less cheerful. At this juncture, a large steamer making for the west, crossed our bows. She seemed steady when compared with us, and I longed to be in her.

The night came on—if all went well, we might reach Sicily before morning. All on board belonged to that country, except myself. They were a good-natured set enough, though their language—which is neither

Spanish nor Italian—is difficult to understand. As the hours wore on, the storm increased; and when the captain, who had throughout shown the greatest coolness and bravery, gave the order to turn towards land, the night was so dark and the sleet so blinding that he had great misgivings as to whether what he saw were really the lights of Marsala or those of another ship.

Fortune favours the brave; and Providence can guide the bark, when the mariners fail. Soon after two in the morning, anchor was dropped. It had, however, very quickly to be weighed again, for the wind was driving the ships in the port against each other. Having gone into a more secure position, we again let go, and this time with better success.

CHAPTER XX.

SICILY.

Marsala—A Beautiful Monstrance—Dining in Sicily—Trapani Palermo—Viva Maria—Santa Rosalia—Montreale—The four thousand Dead—Adieu Sicily.

WHEN the day broke, most of us landed. Marsala was full of monks and priests. The hoods of the former looked quite comfortable at this season. Snow had fallen in the night, and the weather was exceptionally severe. Some of my late comrades in affliction suggested that we should visit a certain monastic church. Built under it, we found a more ancient edifice, containing a skull. After this, we went into the sacristy, and were told that we should see a monstrance of rare beauty. To each was given a lighted candle, and we followed the monk who showed the way. Mounting some steps in the eastern wall, we came upon a platform immediately behind the high altar. A door was opened and the monstrance disclosed. All knelt; for the Blessed Sacrament was there contained. As we raised our eyes to the sacred Host, one of my companions prayed vehemently. And surely the thought of the dangers we had so lately escaped, and of Him who over-rules all, must have crossed the mind of each, when the priest pressed to his lips the monstrance—beautifully wrought, adorned with the figure of the heavenly maid, the infant God, and containing the mystic emblem of His sacred Body.

I determined to go by land to Trapani, and take the chance of brigands, rather than be shut up in the steamer; and as the coach did not start until 10 a.m., I spent the rest of the day in looking at churches—there being little else in Marsala, except the wine manufactory. In the evening I went as usual to dine, but was told at the several hotels and restaurants at which I inquired, that it was quite impossible—everybody in Marsala dines at four; and after that hour all the fires are let out, and no cooking done. If they had told me that before, I would have forgiven them, and conformed to the custom of the country; but this was too bad. "What could I have?" "Eggs and coffee." So with that I was obliged to be contented. I tasted the Marsala wine, now so commonly drunk in England, but could not associate it with what passes under that name in our country.

The next day, mounting a *diligence*, we were driven to Trapani, no very great distance. The worst thing we had to contend against was—not the brigands—but what I have no doubt is thought by many to be more unusual in Sicily—the cold weather. Trapani was *in festa*, the next day being a high festival in honour of the B. V. M. The distance from Trapani to Palermo is pretty considerable; and as the weather was slightly better—and I had no wish to have my ears sent home to my friends with an intimation that so many thousand pounds must be in such a place at such a time—I again took to the sea. One little incident will show the severity of the recent weather: A large steamer belonging to Florio & Co. had been waiting thirteen days in the port of Trapani, while we in our little skiff had crossed from Africa.

Near Palermo, high mountains rise perpendicularly from the sea; the tops generally crowned with a church, or some shrine of a saint. On the same evening of the 8th, we entered the beautiful Bay of Palermo; and the whole extent of the Concha d'Oro was disclosed, most of the mountains being tipped with snow.

Civilization is a pleasure which cannot be thoroughly appreciated, except by those who have lived for some time without its pale. To be in a good European hotel—to be able to dine at what hour one likes—to see people dressed as one is accustomed to see them at home—these are things, the comfort of which I could now fully realize.

Palermo is a remarkably fine city, with streets vying with those of Paris for regularity and length. In addition to this, it is surrounded by mountains, giving it an Alpine appearance.

In very religious Sicily, what can one write about, but churches and church festivals? This was the evening of the Conception of the B. V. M. Opposite San Francisco, was written in illuminated letters, composed of small gas jets, " Viva Maria Immacolata." The church itself was one mass of splendour; silks and satins hung in every direction—glass chandeliers and everything that could in any way reflect the numberless lights—it did not look unlike a ball-room prepared for royalty. When the service, which was accompanied by a full orchestra, was finished, a man gave three cheers for " Maria ! " " Viva Maria ! " " Viva Maria ! " Another, and again the church re-echoed with vivas for Maria. Once more, and whilst the third vociferation was going on, I left.

The cathedral of Santa Rosalia is a large imposing building, studded on its exterior with life-size figures of saints, some pointing towards heaven, as though mutely appealing to the passers-by to look upwards, and not let their minds dwell on the trivial matters of this world. Santa Rosalia is the patroness of Palermo. Her shrine is on a neighbouring hill, and her festival is celebrated in a manner of which Palermo only knows the secret. It is said that the present king stood with open eyes and mouth, when he beheld the wondrous display of fireworks which illuminated the beautiful bay on one of these anniversaries. How gratifying all this must be to the saint!

Montreale is four miles from Palermo. The road thither has, here and there, stations where a few soldiers are picketed. It passes through a perfect bower of oranges and lemons; and after a tolerable ascent, Montreale is reached. The view from a little chapel on a height just above the town is superb; but the great feature is the cathedral—probably the finest Gothic building in this Italian kingdom. It contains the tombs of several Norman kings. Although Sicily is so devoted to religion that it would be difficult to walk a mile in the neighbourhood of habitations without coming across something to bring before the mind, our Faith, our Christian duty, the hereafter life, the one atonement on the Cross, the intense love of those who have forsaken all to follow Christ, despising shame and ignominy, preferring the martyr's crown—yet with all this, we find a people inferior to many others who have not half their privileges, and what is still more singular, externally less reverent and devout. During the celebration of the Divine Office, the people with hardly an exception sit on one chair while they lean forward on a second; even during the elevation, this position is seldom changed.

The Capucin monastery contains a larger burying-place than any other possessed by the order. A monk conducted me below.

We entered a crypt. On each side stood the dead, ghastly to behold, dressed as in life. On the floor lay a number of coffins, containing corpses. Under one I heard a movement; and immediately afterwards, a cat leaped forth. There are several of these animals, I was told, who live down here, to kill the rats, who would otherwise eat the dead.

We walked along corridor after corridor, occasionally stooping to look more particularly at one or other of these silent beings who had anything remarkable about him or her. Several of the women wore crowns.

"Why is this?" I asked.

"They are virgins," replied the monk, "and it is a Sicilian custom."

"But surely the dead are not placed here immediately they die?" I inquired.

"No," said my informant, "they are put in a room in the centre of this building, and there left for a year. They are then brought out, and stood up as you see them."

And so they remain, awaiting the time

when life shall once more vivify these now inanimate forms.

"Here," he said, "is a priest," pointing to a man in cassock and stole. "He died in 1662, and you see his tongue still remains. Saying this, he touched the protruding member. I could not myself see much difference between those who had died in 1662, and those who had died in 1874. Four thousand bodies are supposed to be contained in these catacombs.

On Monday the 13th of December, I embarked in one of Florio's fine steamers, bound for Naples. The voyage was perfect. The Sicilian coast, gilded by the setting sun, looked all that classics or poets could desire, as it faded out of sight. The moon shone out, and traced her rich silver road over the briny deep. Sicily we had left with the setting, Naples we were to see with the rising sun. Vesuvius, surmounted by a thin vapourish smoke, gives to the Bay of Naples its peculiar feature; otherwise it is inferior to that of Palermo.

CHAPTER XXI.

NAPLES.

Population—Vesuvius—The Museo—S. Januarius—Christmas—Cold in Naples—Classical Remains and Solfatara—Avernus—Ascent of Vesuvius—Pompeii—Temple of Isis—Capri—Amalfi—Salerno.

NAPLES, with its teeming population, its life and bustle, its omnibuses and carriages, is a second London or Paris. If the other cities of Italy surpass her in their works of art, the magnificence of their churches, or the sumptuous decoration of their palaces, Naples can at any rate far out-do them in regard to population; and what her citizens lack in quality, she tries to compensate for in their excessive quantity. I think tourists will agree that the Neapolitans are the most degraded race with which they are accustomed to come in contact; although much purged of late, Naples still possesses a population which, for idleness, vice, and cruelty, it would be difficult to match in any other part of the civilized world. And yet with all this, where so fair a country, so genial a climate? A land rich indeed with classic interest, watered by the blood of saint and martyr, trod by the feet of an apostle.

Nature, unable to contain longer the forces which tear asunder the inmost parts of her earth, here belches forth fire and smoke, to the astonishment and consternation of the ignorant, while she baffles the calculations of the wise and prudent. Vesuvius—now smoking as if the subterranean stokers had just piled on fuel upon fuel—now subsiding, until a thin white vapour alone marks the spot where the crater ought to be, is to Naples her greatest, but not her only attraction. Pompeii, Baiæ, Capri, Amalfi, Pæstum, all claim a large share of the traveller's time and attention.

I am glad at last to have found a place

where the weather (the resort of all who do not know what to say,) has been superseded as a topic of conversation. "How is Vesuvius?" follows the usual "How do you do?" in Naples. "So and so thought he saw flame last night," etc. The great ambition of all English and Americans residing temporarily in this neighbourhood, is to see an eruption; and as such an event seemed just now somewhat likely, the mountain claimed even more than its usual share of notice. Some would speak of it as though it were an interesting patient, and say that Professor Palmieri (the scientific observer who lives up there) had felt its pulse that morning, and thought the case looked more hopeful.

It would be difficult to say of Naples what has not already been said. It has, in fact, been done to death. Everybody knows everything about it; and unless it can be put in a very new light indeed, nobody cares to hear anything more. My remarks, therefore, shall be confined to the narrowest possible limits. The only important monument in the city is the Museo, interesting on account of the treasures that have been brought there from Pompeii and Herculaneum. There is actually the bread, baked and unbaked, just as it was left, on the fearful night of the tragedy; the beds and baths; the oil lamps and their stands;—all in fact that was needed for the well-being of a Roman family of the first century, even down to the drugs and the surgical instruments.

On the 16th of December I went to the cathedral with some friends, upon a report that the blood of S. Januarius was about to liquify. The chapel in which the miracle was to have been performed is an octagonal building, richly decorated, on the right hand side as one enters the cathedral. It contains some half-dozen altars, at which masses were following one another with the rapidity of Metropolitan trains; and was crowded with people, who were mostly seated, and seemed quite indifferent to the

Holy Mysteries which were being celebrated all around them. The blood of S. Januarius was in a glass case, and was then solid. Crowds flocked up to kiss it; and the priest whose business it was to carry it round and present it to each had but little rest. As our party were foreigners, we were admitted to a reserved part within the altar rails; and there kneeling down, the sacred relic was pressed to my lips, and the sign of the cross made over me with it. Why did it not liquify? This was the question my friends were beginning to ask. "When will it liquify?" said one of them to a pious Neapolitan hard by. The native looked at him in astonishment; and then said gravely, " That depends upon the grace of S. Januarius." High mass was celebrated; but the saint was obdurate. A Te Deum was chanted, with fiddles and all kinds of instruments, the Cardinal Archbishop assisting pontifically; but still S. Januarius showed no sign. His statue was promenaded about the church; but alas! all to no effect. So we had to leave without seeing what we had come for.

Christmas has been heralded in with all popular signs of rejoicing, and little boys have been giving vent to their feelings by letting off fireworks in the public streets. It is very cheering to think that they should be so grateful, and mindful of the blessings which are as at this time showered upon them; yet if they could find some means other than squibs and crackers, of expressing their appreciation, it would be a great boon to those who, like myself, have a decided objection to sharp and sudden noises in unexpected places.

The new year has come, and to-day, the sixth of January, a hard frost covers the face of the country, and icicles are hanging from the fountains in the public gardens. Of course such a thing had never happened before for a hundred years at least! A friend of mine arrived in Naples two consecutive winters, and on each occasion found it white with snow. The first time, he believed the statement that nothing similar had ever occurred in the memory of living man; but on hearing the same asseveration the second year, his faith began to be a little shaken.

From San Martino a glorious view of the town and bay is to be had. The ancient monastery—still celebrated for its liqueur—possesses a chapel richer in pictures, marbles, and lapis lazuli than any the great city can boast.

It is not, however, in the town that the treasures of Naples are to be sought. She may be said, in a word, to lie in her environs. The road which conducts to Baiæ, after passing the Tomb of Virgil, enters a long tunnel lighted with gas; and in due course reaches Pozzuoli. It was here that the great Apostle of the Gentiles landed in chains, when appealing from the local courts of Judea to the Imperial power in Rome.

Pozzuoli still retains in good preservation a fine amphitheatre and the ruins of the

Temple of Jupiter Serapis. In its vicinity is the small volcano of Solfatara. The steam is seen rising from the earth as the traveller approaches, and when quite near, he will perceive that it comes out of the side of a rock in puffs, like the vapour from a locomotive engine, and making much the same noise.

Farther along the high road, and turning off to the right, is Avernus; and the old quotation, "*Facilis descensus Averni,*" is on everybody's lips. It is said that the lake has lost much of its sombre appearance since Virgil's time, through the removal of trees.

In regaining the high road, Monte Nuova is seen to the right. This strange mountain came up in a day, during an eruption in the sixteenth century. Then comes Baiæ, situated on its bay of surpassing loveliness, and containing the ruins of five temples. Still farther on, are the hundred chambers of Nero, the Piscina Mirabilis, and Cape Misenum—the latter celebrated for its view. The return to Naples completes a hard day's work, more exhausting to the mind than to the body. To have brought before one, associations which have in most cases lain dormant since leaving school or college, as well as places whose names are familiar as household words—scenes which show the wonderful working of nature, and beauties transcending all description—such a combination can but produce a sense of fatigue and confusion. I visited these places with an Oxford acquaintance, and felt so taken back to University life, that if we had had caps and gowns at hand, we should certainly have put them on to dine in that evening.

The ascent of Vesuvius generally occupies a day. The road winding up the mountain frequently crosses and re-crosses a stream of lava, the under part of which is hard and glistening like polished metal, while the upper part forms itself into all sorts of fantastic shapes. As the observatory is approached, the different issues of lava can be distinctly traced—1858, 1866, 1872. Beyond the observatory I did not go. The ascent is very fatiguing, and the fumes of sulphur—if the wind blows in a particular direction—too strong to be agreeable. Smoke, tinged with red, was issuing from the crater at the time of our visit, and the day too cloudy to give any hopes of a good view.

Pompeii, the great relic of Roman civilization, lies not far from the base of the volcano. It contains streets, houses, shops, courts of justice, temples, theatres (tragic and comic), and a forum. If the public buildings could only be restored, the houses roofed in, and the streets peopled with their ancient inhabitants, nothing would be wanting to produce in all its perfection a town of the first century. As it is, it affords a more practical study of the manners and customs, the habits and the amusements of the Romans, than can be obtained elsewhere. The streets at present have a deserted appearance, and the frescos are fast fading under the influence of exposure to light and damp. The temple of Isis, built for Egyptian worship, used to contain a speaking oracle. The manner in which this jugglery was managed is very simple; a hole through the centre of the pedestal on which the oracle stood, corresponding with one in the image itself, and a concealed place beneath, whence the priest could speak, was all the apparatus necessary to deceive the popular mind of Pompeii. Round about the temples are the altars, *still* stained with the blood of the sacrifices offered eighteen hundred years ago. The bodies of the men and women that have been exhumed are now placed in a museum. Some died quietly; whilst others—from their expression—must have suffered much before death came to their relief.

Herculaneum is less interesting than Pompeii, the difficulties of excavating it being much greater. Castellamare di Stabia has a population if possible outvying that of Naples in dirt and degradation. Sorrento, with its bowers of oranges, looks charming on a fine day, but in winter is too damp for a residence.

I joined a party bound for Capri. We left in a small boat, which first made for the Blue Grotto. The entrance is very low, all being obliged to lie down in the boat whilst passing under it. The water inside is of the deepest blue; and one of our number said that no picture he had ever seen could give a just representation of the colouring in the grotto. Would that I were a poet, that I might do justice to Capri! "Heaven-born isle, whence didst thou spring?" I know is a right beginning, but I can't get on. "Un pezzo di cielo caduto per terra" might be said of Capri, but the Neapolitans have no right to claim it for their city. The last fortnight of February I dreamed away life in this little rocky island. The weather for the whole period was nearly cloudless—the sea one mass of ever-changing blue—and the foliage and flowers like a perennial spring. Seldom were we in the house—always exploring some fresh portion of our island, or climbing some fresh peak.

The Capresi appear not to have much idea of British courage. One of our party, a brave Scot, going for a stroll before breakfast, met with a pigeon; and stopping for a moment to admire the bird, was accosted by an islander, who, attributing his movements to fear, said with an encouraging air, "Don't be afraid, it won't hurt you." When out later in the day, we held a council of war before venturing to pass a hen on our path!

The streets of Capri are narrow, and not unlike those of an Eastern city. There is now a road to Anacapri, the former picturesque flight of steps being still used by pedestrians. The women carry burdens on their heads, and are remarkable for their beauty. It is said that the Greek type is discernible at Anacapri, and the Roman at Capri. There are remains of several villas built by the Emperor Tiberius, who at one time lived here. There is also a point called the "Salto di Tiberio," from whence there is a perpendicular dip to the sea of about 1,000 feet. Tiberius is said to have thrown his wives over here, when no longer having any use for them.

The number of beggars in the island is something incredible. Nearly all the grown people and all the children, with hardly an exception, beg. With them, putting out the hand on meeting a stranger is a kind of second nature. Even walking on the top of the hotel (the houses here have flat roofs, as in the East) I have often heard beggars calling at us from their houses, a hundred, or a couple of hundred yards off. Perhaps they expected one of us to call upon them in the course of the day, and leave our gratuity.

Faith and fireworks are closely connected in the minds of the Capresi. With them the Host would not be considered to have received its proper homage and devotion were its elevation not announced by the simultaneous explosion of a volley of squibs. The Sanctus also receives great additional *éclat* when sung in concert with these same fiery accompaniments.

The day for parting came, and we left the island with a sorry heart, took a boat, and passing some of the superb scenery of the northern part of the Gulf of Salerno, arrived the same evening at Amalfi, which is completely shut in by high mountains.

I had always heard of this as the most beautiful spot in the neighbourhood of Naples, and it is customary for those who visit it to get out of describing it, by saying that words are completely powerless to do it justice; or by simply telling the enquirer, that "there is but one Amalfi in the world." If Amalfi were a Spanish name, I would undertake to refute this assertion by a careful study of the map of South America, but being in Italy, perhaps there *is* only one Amalfi in the world. After all, this does not say much, as it is a peculiarity common to many places. Once a lady got a little farther and talked about colouring;—very safe, as all parts of the Gulf of Naples and Salerno are famed for their fine colouring; and to do Amalfi justice, it is no exception to the general rule. But when a place has to keep up such a tremendous reputation as this has, it is most likely that people will be disappointed. The town is one of the dirtiest in Italy, and is filled with beggars, who seize hold of the passers-by, in order to attract their attention to some loathsome wound. The day of our arrival being the last of the Carnival, the streets were filled with ladies and gentlemen in masks;—what amusement there can be in walking about looking like a fool, I leave for those who do it to decide. The cathedral, which is an effective building, if only from its position, contains the body of S. Andrew, brought from the East in the middle ages.

The city of Ravello is distant a mile and a half from here, and to get up to it a succession of steps have to be mounted for nearly the whole way. Its cathedral contains a very fine ambo from which to read the gospel; it is, however, placed on the epistle side, that the bishop may see it from his throne.

From Amalfi to Salerno is a drive of two hours. It is finer than the road between Castellamare and Sorrento, though in the same style. Salerno is a town of considerable importance, being the seat of an Archbishop Metropolitan, as well as of many high civil dignitaries. The tourist will know it, from its being the usual starting point for Pæstum. The wonderful temples of that place are believed to date from before 600 B.C. A picture I saw of one of them reminded me of the Madeleine at Paris. We did not care to drive for fifty miles (twenty-five there and twenty-five back) through a dangerous, or *quasi*-dangerous country, in order to be gratified by the sight of three ruins, but preferred spending our time in Salerno.

If Amalfi possesses the shrine of S. Andrew, Salerno, not to be out-done, boasts that of S. Matthew. It is contained in a subterranean chapel, one mass of marble. To visit the shrines of two apostles on two successive days was a privilege of which I hope we were thoroughly sensible. Some steps took us into the cathedral, a perfect Basilica, containing ambones—the gospel one being on the epistle side, as at Ravello, and for the same reason.

Although the early part of March, and a seaside place, Salerno was hot, the sun having attained great power even at this early period.

On the 6th of March, our Capri party left for Rome.

CHAPTER XXII.

ROME TO MENTONE.

Rome—Two Remarkable Events—The Colosseum—Its present use—S. Peter's and S. Paul's—Orvieto and Siena—Italian Pictures—Pisa—Genoa—Adieu Italy.

IF it would be difficult to say of Naples what has not been said before, how much more so must it be of Rome! In these days, people prefer gaining their information about the principal cities of Italy by personal inspection, rather than taking it second-hand, upon the authority of others. It is so easy to join a Cook or a Gaze: in less than sixty hours from the time of leaving London, you can be in Rome; in a few days you can gaze (this is not meant for a pun) at all the principal sights of the Eternal City; another sixty hours, and you are back in London. To do all this, one need run no more risk than in travelling the same distance in England or Scotland; nor need one know a word of any foreign language, nor undergo the slightest privation in the way of food or lodging. All that is required, is to pay so many pounds, and everything will be done for you.

Two remarkable events have happened in Rome since I was last here (in 1869); the one political, the other ecclesiastical. The former has, perhaps, had the greatest immediate effect upon the city; it has made her the capital of Italy, and has given to her citizens that freedom which is the due of an enlightened people. The latter has separated Church and State, beyond the possibility of an understanding. How can an Infallible Pontiff negotiate on terms of equality with a mortal and erring king? And how can a mortal and erring king, with history and contemporary facts before him, commit his people to the judgment and dictates of a—so-called—Infallible Pontiff?

The general aspect of the city has been much altered by the events alluded to. There are no longer to be seen the gorgeous equipages which, in former days, conveyed cardinal or archbishop to and from church or duomo; no longer does the Holy Father drive through the streets of Rome, with his half-dozen of cream-coloured horses. The very monks, with their picturesque and varied dresses, are fast disappearing; and even the beggars begin to follow suit! Although many may shed a romantic or an æsthetic tear over the ashes of the past, yet few will deny that the city is more prosperous, now that things pertaining to this world, and things pertaining to the next, each have their separate head and officers.

The Colosseum has been somewhat altered by the removal of certain religious shrines from its interior, and by excavating part of it below the then existing level. This building commemorates the last great work of the Cæsars. The festivals with which it was inaugurated lasted some hundred days.

Gladiators and wild animals here fought and died, in the presence of nearly one hundred thousand spectators; even naval contests could be produced, by flooding certain portions of the arena; and during the persecutions of the Church, many Christians here mingled their expiring cries with those of the gladiators and the wild beasts. In the middle ages, the Colosseum was sadly neglected. At one time it was a soap-boiling establishment; and frequently, in the course of its existence, it has been the rendezvous of the worst characters, who would take up their habitation here, and remain unmolested for long periods. About the middle of the eighteenth century, the interior of the edifice was consecrated to the Passion of Christ—a very appropriate designation, considering how often the blood of martyrs had there flowed. Recent popes protected it from farther ruin, by building buttresses to keep up any part which looked as if likely to fall in. The latest use to which the Colosseum has been put, is to afford a tolerably quiet and secluded retreat for lovers who like moonlight walks. It is the fashion to say now, that the Colosseum, like "fair Melrose," to be seen "aright," must be seen by "the pale moonlight;" so this forms a good excuse for young ladies and gentlemen to be hovering about there whenever the moon sheds her pale lustre over the venerable ruin. One instance of the fatal question having been put and answered in the vicinity of the building has happened within the limited circle of my acquaintance.

On the Arch of Titus is a bas-relief of the seven-branched candlestick used in the Temple worship at Jerusalem. This is, I believe, the only representation which gives to the curious in matters of Jewish history any authentic idea of the nature of that candlestick.

The four churches of Rome, *par excellence*, are S. Peter's, S. Paul's, S. Mary's, and S. John's. The first of these is stated to be the largest in the world. It was commenced in 1450 A.D., over the remains of a more ancient edifice; and it was at first intended to build it in the shape of a Greek cross; but this idea was subsequently abandoned, and the form of the Latin cross adopted. Its size and gigantic proportions are its chief features. Under the high altar is the shrine of S. Peter, and a quantity of lights are kept burning in its vicinity. S. Paul's—outside the walls—is in the opinion of many the finest church in Italy, and I am inclined to agree with those who hold this view. It is a nineteenth century edifice; and, if the above supposition is correct, helps to prove that nothing was ever done better than it is in the present day. I know it is customary to say that no living artist can equal a Titian or a Raphael, but how much of this may be due to a desire to say the correct thing, and how much to genuine conviction, is an open question.

Many stories are current about the very indifferent air with which our Transatlantic cousins treat the Eternal City. One of them is said to have boasted that he could "do it in a day;" another that he thought it "a fine place, only the public buildings were rather out of repair." The following, however, is the best. A lady, on being interrogated, on her return to the States, as to whether she had been at Rome, was beginning to reply in the negative, when her daughter, coming to her relief, said,—

"Oh! yes, mamma; don't you remember? That was the place where we bought the bad stockings!"

Orvieto and Siena are towns which tourists very often miss, as they rush from Florence to Rome, or *vice versâ*. They should, however, by all means, be seen. It is true Orvieto contains nothing but the façade of its cathedral, but then that façade is the finest in the world, for mosaics and marbles. The interior, composed of alternate black and white blocks of marble, has too sombre an appearance, and contrasts unfavourably with the rich west front. Siena is much in the same style; the interior far superior to Orvieto, while the façade falls short of its more southern rival.

Picture galleries in Italy have a great family likeness—they help us to form some idea of the Italian mind of the middle and later middle ages. That of Siena may be taken as a very fair type;—nineteen-twentieths of the pictures are devoted to the delineation of saints and Madonnas. Christ is seldom represented, except as an infant, or dead. To the Italian, there seems to be nothing in His mission worth recording but His birth and His death. The numberless works of mercy which are recorded as having been done by the Saviour—feeding the hungry, healing the sick, raising the dead, preaching to the unenlightened—which, one would have thought, ought to have furnished so prolific a subject for the Christian brush—are here almost entirely ignored; and Christ dying, Christ dead, Christ an infant—is all that we see.

The monuments of Pisa are contained in small compass—two hours, and one can see all. The Campanile, or Leaning Tower, was, from all appearances, intended to be a perpendicular building. When partially completed, the foundation gave way; the remaining portion was then added, and the effort to regain the perpendicular as much as possible is seen in the present curved outline. Since my last visit here, the railway to Genoa has been completed; and although the scenery between Spezia and Sestri is lost by this arrangement, an immense amount of time is saved. So much tunnelling is done at certain parts of this line, that one might almost fancy oneself in an underground railway. La Superba—the Italian epithet for Genoa—was exceedingly windy when we arrived. The chief attractions here, are, as usual in Italy, churches and palaces. Santa Maria dell' Annunziata equals for gorgeous decoration anything in the kingdom.

A few hours' railway brought us to San Remo, a great resort of invalids. A little farther on, is Bordighera, which supplies the palms for the Roman churches, on Palm Sunday. A little farther on still is the French frontier; and half a mile beyond that, Mentone. Adieu, Italy!

CHAPTER XXIII.

MENTONE TO LONDON.

Snow at Mentone—Gambling at Monaco—Nice—Cannes—Hyères—Marseilles—Arles and Nîmes—Avignon—Grenoble—Chambéry—Aix-les-Bains—Geneva—Easter with the Old Catholics—The Castle of Chillon—Paris—The Thames—London at last.

I HAD been told that Mentone would be too hot at the end of March; but instead of finding it so, we thought it, on the contrary, a great deal too cold. Snow fell frequently on the 20th and 21st, and for some days an east wind was blowing, enough to cut any Christian in two. Such weather had not been experienced during the whole winter, said the hotel-keeper and the waiter. This, of course, we believed implicitly, as the statements of interested people are always so reliable. With regard to the two bays, it is said that the eastern one has a temperature several degrees higher than the western. We were living in the east bay, and if this is the case, I should not have cared to change into the west, just at that time. As a winter resort, it is, however, probably as good as any along the Riviera. The southern vegetation found on this coast proves that the weather, taken as a whole, cannot be very severe; but to say that snow and ice are *never* seen, is about as correct as to say that *all* November days in England are invariably foggy.

Between Mentone and Nice lies the little Principality of Monaco. It contains gambling tables similar to those formerly used in Germany. The smallest piece that can be risked at Roulette is five francs; and the maximum sum which can be played is, I believe, nine thousand francs. On the Trente et Quarante table, only gold is allowed, and the maximum is twelve thousand francs. About a minute is given for persons to place their stakes; in another, the play is decided, and hundreds of pounds may have to change hands. No sooner has this been settled, than the players put on for the next turn: and so they go on, hour after hour. Suicides are frequently reported as the result of gambling. They are not, perhaps, all due entirely to Monaco. Take the following instance:—A. has lost his fortune by lending it to Turkey, or by taking up the securities of some worthless South American Republic. He knows himself to be a ruined man, realizes a few hundreds, the proceeds of his depreciated bonds, and determines to go to Monaco, retrieve all, or commit suicide. Such a case could hardly be laid entirely to the account of Monaco; and it is to be feared that it is not an uncommon one.

Nice is the most fashionable of all the Riviera watering-places, and is frequented by those who cannot do without the song and the dance. Those who love the beauties of nature, and care little for close theatres and heated rooms, will find Mentone or San Remo better suited to their temperaments.

Cannes, about fifteen miles from Nice and double that distance from Mentone, is next reached. Opposite is the island where was confined the man with the iron mask; and more recently, the scapegoat of the last French war—M. Bazaine.

Some hours of railway, and Toulon is reached. A short branch line takes the traveller to Hyères, containing beautiful palms and charming gardens. Marseilles was our next halt. Those who come here should not fail to mount as far as Notre Dame de la Garde, whence a magnificent view of the town, the harbour, and the islands can be obtained.

The train skirts a large inlet of the sea as it steers north-west for Arles. The Roman remains (both here and at Nîmes) generally attract less attention than they deserve: the enormous amphitheatre is more than a quarter of a mile in circumference, and in good preservation; there are also the remains of a theatre of considerable size. The same day, we went on to Nîmes: the amphitheatre here, although not quite so large as that at Arles, is in a wonderful state of preservation. The performances in the Roman times were gratis, and are supposed to have occupied the greater part of the day. The small dens under the amphitheatre, which some thought were the permanent habitations of the wild beasts, our guide explained, could only have been used for their temporary reception, immediately prior to the contests; for, as he wisely remarked, "animals accustomed to African heat would not live very long in these nasty damp places." The amphitheatre at Arles was fortified by the Saracens, when they located themselves in this part of the country. The present use of that building, as well as of the one here, is for the representation of *quasi* bull-fights: a bull is let into the arena; and those who feel disposed go in also, and there display their agility and their daring to an admiring public. Accidents of course are not unfrequent; but these seem in no way to deter others from following the same foolhardy course. The bulls are never killed; and the whole of the entertainment consists in the above.

Avignon comes next on the northward route. Here the true successors of S. Peter so long found a refuge, when Rome was in the hands of apostates and antipopes. The papal palace is a substantial building; and the cathedral, like all we had seen since leaving Italy, plain and unpretending when compared with the gorgeous churches of that country. We followed the Paris line as far as Valence, then turned east into Dauphiny; passed through a valley, and, after four and a quarter hours, reached Grenoble, surrounded by mountains now covered with snow, which gave it something the appearance of Palermo. It is clean, and well built. All the French provincial towns resemble each other more or less; for the aim of each is to be like Paris. After Grenoble, we came to Chambèry, so long the capital of the House of Savoy. For this reason, it is far more like an Italian than a French town; and many of its churches—especially the cathedral —have the warm colouring of Italy. A little beyond Chambèry is Aix-les-Bains, a watering-place much frequented by the French in the summer. At the time of our visit (11th of April), it had a most forsaken appearance. Many of the shops were closed, the hotels empty; and besides this, snow was falling fast. The railway to Geneva follows the course of the Rhone, and passes through fine scenery. Before we were allowed to leave French territory, a young man came round, and wanted to know our names.

At Geneva, we spent the last four days of the Holy Week. The large cathedral, close to the station, which formerly belonged to the Roman Catholics, has now fallen into the hands of the Old Catholics. These latter, as is very well known, seceded on account of their not being able to receive that singular doctrine of Papal Infallibility. We attended some of their services on Good Friday and Easter Day. They certainly have made one great improvement: what is said, is said in the vernacular, and not in a dead language. Otherwise, they do not differ much, in doctrine or practice, from the body they have left. Their ceremonial was poor, and by no means equalled what we are accustomed to see in some of our advanced churches at home.

Geneva is a sort of tourists' head-quarters. Everything that they can want is sold here; and the facilities for lodging strangers are perhaps more extensive than anywhere else. If natural scenery is sought, the tourist should not remain in Geneva; but take train or steamer, and away to the other end of the lake! This we did, and spent a very pleasant fortnight not half a mile from the Castle of Chillon. What lovely scenery! The Dent du Midi, covered by its virgin snow, the mountains on the opposite side rising perpendicularly from the lake, and the castle nestling hard by—the castle which Byron stooped to extol.

We left on the 1st of May, and being detained some time at Dijon, wandered about the quiet streets, for it was past midnight. At Paris, I visited for the first time the "tombeau de Napoléon." What an idol for the French people to worship! We turned in, to see the pictures, at the Palais d'Industrie. There was Gustave Doré's latest, the Triumphal Entry into Jerusalem: those who strewed the palms had on the brightest and the cleanest of dresses—the palms were the greenest of the green;—so unlike what we are generally told about the Eastern vegetation, and the filthiness of the dresses of the common people.

Boulogne-sur-Mer! We were now almost in sight of perfidious Albion. The steamer for London left at ten at night; and early the next morning, the traditional fog being so thick, we dropped anchor off Gravesend, and waited until it cleared. After an absence of nine months and nine days, I looked again on my native shores. As we pass the military academy at Woolwich, I thought I had seen something like that elsewhere, and found I was thinking of the Escorial. The fog was now so much better that a sailor thought he saw the time, as we passed Greenwich. It was not, however, London proper yet, only Wapping; and we land at St. Katherine's Wharf. The Tower comes next; then Thames Street; next London Bridge: but it was only when the gilt cross on the dome of the metropolitan church reflected back the rays of the morning sun, that I could say, "My task is done,—this is London indeed!"

CHAPTER XXIV.

STATISTICS AND FINANCES.

As it may be interesting to some, to know the distances travelled in this recent tour, and the expenses incidental to the same, I have in conclusion subjoined the following remarks and tables. From the time of leaving London to the time of returning thither, occupied two hundred and eighty-three days; the distance traversed was, in round numbers, six thousand miles; and the amounts paid for railways, steamers, *diligences*, etc., £40, being at the rate of £6 13s. 4d. per thousand miles, or 13s. 4d. per hundred miles. The journey may be farther subdivided into three sections:—

	Miles.	Cost.	
		£ s. d.	
London to Gibraltar	1,900	12 10 0	
Gibraltar to Naples	2,000	15 0 0	Second class rail.
Naples to London	1,800	10 0 0	
Sundry excursions	300	2 10 0	
Total	6,000	40 0 0	

From this it will be seen that the dearest mileage is in the African, and the cheapest in the Italian section. The following shows the fares per hundred miles, charged by the railways in the following countries.

	1st class.	2nd class.	3rd class.	
	s. d.	s. d.	s. d.	
France				These are only
Algeria	16 0	12 0	8 0	approximate, as
Spain				different lines in the
Switzerland	15 0	10 0	7 6	same country have
Italy	13 0	9 0	6 4	varying charges.

In the first three, sixty-six pounds of luggage are allowed free; while in Switzerland and Italy, *all* luggage has to be paid for.

Diligence travelling in Spain is being fast superseded. The railway is open to Granada; and projects for a through line to Galicia, which have long been in contemplation, are now in a great measure realized.

In Morocco, there are no roads. Excepting for the seaport towns, all communication is kept up by means of horses, mules, or camels. From Tangier to Fez would take six days. Tents are taken, and about thirty miles ridden *per diem*; a soldier of the imperial guard always escorts the party. There are in Tangier trustworthy Arabs who will organize parties; their charges are about £1 a day, horses, food, lodging, and everything included.

In Algeria, a great deal of travelling is done by *diligence*; the French having made good roads in many parts of the colony. The charges vary; but, on the whole, would be about the same as first-class railway fare. From Batna to Biskra, the usual *coupé* charge is twenty-five francs; and the distance seventy-five miles. As there was talk of a competition when we went, the fare had been reduced to eighteen francs. On our return,—a rival van having really been set up—it was farther reduced to eight francs for the interior, and twelve for the *coupé*. Those who wish to visit the more remote oases, inexpensively, should join a caravan. See remarks in Chapter XVII.

The Regency of Tunis, excepting the capital, is very little visited. What has been said of Morocco would, in a great measure, apply here; though this country is not quite so backward with regard to roads, and even has a few miles of railway near the capital.

Coaching is still a good deal resorted to in Sicily, owing to the mountainous nature of the country, and the difficulties in the way of making railroads.

Very varying indeed are the passengers' fares charged by vessels sailing in the Mediterranean. In many instances they depend upon bargain, and are nearly always quite as dear—and in some cases dearer—than journeying the same distance by land. The larger have three classes—first, second, and third; first and second class passengers having equal privileges as regards walking on the quarterdeck.

Hotel expenses vary even more than do the charges by the steamers, and in nine cases out of ten depend entirely upon what arrangements the traveller has made previous to entering the hotel. Assuming that he never has anything until he knows what it is to cost—that he speaks with tolerable fluency the language of the country—that he invariably makes his own bargain instead of letting himself fall into the hands of *commissionaires*—he need not, under these circumstances, pay more, on an average, than from five to six shillings a day in Spain and Italy, and from six to seven in Algeria. If, however, the above rules are not followed, from fifty to a hundred per cent. above these charges should be reckoned upon. Tunis and Biskra are rather dearer; the accommodation for travellers in both places being limited.

The number of different places slept in during the two hundred and eighty-three days of travel (exclusive of nights passed in trains, carriages, or steam-ships) was fifty-nine, or, on an average, a fresh one in every five days. The number of places where halt was made to see or admire any particular person or thing, was eighty-six, or one in about every three and a half days. The number of countries visited was six; and in five cases the capital was seen. I wish I could complete this list by giving the number of people met with in the celebrated two hundred and eighty-three days, but I am afraid that this is beyond the power of my memory.

Luggage is always the great trouble with which the tourist has to be incessantly contending. If too little is taken, there are the regrets that useful things are lying useless at home, whilst fresh ones have to be bought. If, on the other hand, the traveller has with him a thing he does not want, he bitterly regrets the day when he increased his troubles — already too grievous to be borne—by this additional piece of *impedimenta*. For a two hundred and eighty-three days' tour, I would recommend a good-sized portmanteau, containing an ordinary outfit, with changes suitable to hot and cold weather; the weight of this should not, if possible, exceed sixty-six pounds (that quantity being free in several countries). It is only to be taken to the hotel when a long stay is contemplated; at other times it is to be left at the railway station, or at the town where the tourist temporarily takes up his head-quarters. Besides this portmanteau there should be a small hand-bag with a strap, so that it could be swung over the shoulder—containing brushes, combs, slippers, soap, sponge, and night-shirt, and as much clean linen as can be got into it. This should always accompany the traveller wherever he goes; and with this he ought to be able to dispense with his portmanteau for two or three days.

Money should be taken in the form of circular notes, and care exercised not to carry the money of one country into another.

By a decree issued soon after the abdication of Queen Isabella, the Spanish peseta, or franc, was to consist of one hundred centimes. The decimal system has not, however, taken with the people, and they still persist in counting by their reales—value twopence-halfpenny each. The number of false coins circulating in the Peninsula is very considerable. I have heard it asserted that twenty-five per cent. of the one hundred reales gold pieces are base; they are not, however, entirely worthless, as they are made of silver or platinum, and have a tolerably thick coating of gold, being so perfect that it is only when they are rubbed for some time against a rough surface that the white colour of the silver becomes perceptible.

The Moorish money is almost entirely bronze. Silver coins are rare, and gold still more scarce. The Europeans generally use the Spanish money for large sums.

In Algeria, the French coinage is now almost universal. In Bougie, there is a

Kabyle coin which passes for half a franc; but it was refused in Setif.

Tunis has a good and complete money system. There are small gold coins of the value of about half-a-crown; silver coins ranging from under a penny, upwards; and copper ones beginning at sums too low to specify.

It takes some time to realize that the filthy bits of paper which—if seen in any other country than Italy—would have been put down as having come from the gutter, really represent values of various amounts. But when we have done this, and have forgotten that the change we take may have just passed through the hands of a scarlet-fever or small-pox patient, and that paper conveys infection far more readily than gold or silver, the currency of Italy may be looked upon with some degree of favour; it is so easy to carry, and makes no noise when paid away. I have often heard it said, and with some show of reason, that it is a foolish thing for a country to waste its resources in buying precious metals to manufacture into money, when paper will do just as well, at any rate for all internal purposes.

But this is more a question for Finance Ministers, and persons holding Portfolios, than for ordinary mortals; so I will turn to the best manner and demeanour for the traveller to assume, when brought into contact with Spaniards, Arabs, or Italians. With the first, he should always remember that every Spaniard is a grandee; and in all his intercourse with him, should never lose sight of this important fact,—the traveller himself is of course also a grandee —encountering a Spaniard is like knight meeting knight.

With Arabs, the best demeanour is calm, self-possessed serenity. They will not be hurried, and if the traveller should be called upon to wait two hours while they arrange something which anybody else could do in half of one, he will not hasten matters by talking: they will simply leave off what they are doing to talk too. The best thing under such circumstances, if one cannot do what is required oneself, is to sit down cross-legged, with folded hands, the countenance of a Stoic, and eyes turned towards heaven.

The Italian likes familiarity; he is all life and gaiety, seldom depressed for long, and likes best those who are as light-hearted as he is himself.

The following is from the *Standard* of May 19th, and relates to events mentioned in Chapter XIII. :—

ORAN, *May* 18th.

"The criminal proceedings against the murderer and bandit Bousian-el-Kalai and his band, who were the terror of this province, were brought to a conclusion to-day, after having lasted for ten days. The prisoners, twelve in number, were accused of having committed no less than fifty-six crimes, viz., five murders, twelve attempts at murder, thirty-five robberies, and three attempts at robbery. Bousian-el-Kalai, the captain of the band, was condemned to death; his lieutenant, a Mahometan priest named Si Kaddour Ben Hamida, and eight other prisoners, all Arabs, were condemned to imprisonment, with hard labour, for life; and two of the prisoners, a Cadi and a Frenchman named Graillat, were acquitted. The jury took five hours to consider their verdict."

THE END.

www.ingramcontent.com/pod-product-compliance
Lightning Source LLC
Chambersburg PA
CBHW032053220426
43664CB00008B/987